I belong only to myself

The Life and Writings of Leda Rafanelli

AK
PRESS
EDINBURGH · OAKLAND · BALTIMORE

I belong only to myself

The Life and Writings of Leda Rafanelli

Andrea Pakieser

I Belong Only to Myself: The Life and Writings of Leda Rafanelli
© 2014 Andrea Pakieser (editor).

This edition © 2014 AK Press (Oakland, Edinburgh, Baltimore).
ISBN: 978-1-84935-195-9 | 978-1-84935-196-6
Library of Congress Control Number: 2014940776

AK Press	AK Press
674-A 23rd Street	PO Box 12766
Oakland, CA 94612	Edinburgh EH8 9YE
USA	Scotland
www.akpress.org	www.akuk.com
akpress@akpress.org	ak@akedin.demon.co.uk

The above addresses would be delighted to provide you with the latest AK Press distribution catalog, which features the several thousand books, pamphlets, zines, audio and video products, and stylish apparel published and/or distributed by AK Press. Alternatively, visit our websites for the complete catalog, latest news, and secure ordering.

Cover design by Kate Khatib | manifestor.org/design
Printed in the USA on acid-free paper.

CONTENTS

Acknowledgments

To Fiamma Chessa, for sharing her knowledge on Leda Rafanelli and the Italian anarchist movement: thank you for your patient explanations and your warm welcome at the archives. Ti ringrazio di cuore per tutto.

To my friends who are family and my family who are friends: thank you for the moral, emotional, and intellectual support, with a special thanks to Sofya, Linda, and Dirk for their help and feedback on earlier drafts.

To the staff and editors at AK: thank you for your insight and guidance in pulling this project together.

Je voudrais dédier ce livre à mes nièces, Violet et Ivy, deux belles âmes pleines de joie.

Pas de règles pour la vie, mes filles, donc vivez ce que vous avez à vivre.

CHAPTER I
Introduction: Social Sketches

The factory's daughter

One evening, toward the end of a long day of hard work, a commotion arose in the spinning mill. Rosa, a young worker about twenty years old, was carrying a bucket of boiling water when she suddenly came down with labor pains. All of the other women workers knew that Rosa had been seduced by their boss one autumn night, behind the heap of baskets filled with silkworm cocoons.

The boss had been flirting with the young worker for a long time. He wanted nothing more than to possess her, to make her his lover for a little while and then abandon her. That fateful autumn evening he had led her behind the mountain of baskets overflowing with golden cocoons: the source of his riches also happened to be handy for hiding their lovemaking from the vigilant eyes of the factory guards. And Rosa, stunned by his kisses and caresses, gave in to his desires...

She had returned to that spot several times, during the evenings, after work, and she was soon with child. When her figure took on the contours of her pregnancy, the boss no longer wanted anything to do with her.

And on that scorching day in July, Rosa gave birth, right there in the factory. Her fellow workers, who knew what had happened and sympathized with her, cared for her with the utmost concern. But two hours after the baby was born, Rosa died: her frail body, worn out from the exhausting work in the spinning mill, was unable to survive the stress.

The newborn was a little girl. And the dead woman's workmates made sure that this poor baby, an orphan from birth, was not handed over to the hospital.

They named her Maria and took turns looking after her. As an infant, Maria nursed from the breasts of all of the working mothers, and as a young child, she made the rounds of all of their homes, eating at all of their tables, sleeping in all of their beds, tenderly calling all of the women who worked at the spinning mill "mama." Until the age of ten or eleven, she spent her days playing with the other children, many of whom were her milk brothers and sisters, in the steep back alleys of the little village which stood in the shadow of the spinning mill where she had been born. And she grew up healthy and strong, with the special nickname of *the factory's daughter*.

—

While still a young girl, the factory's daughter also started working at the plant. She settled in permanently with an old woman who had since left the mill and now stayed at home in the working-class neighborhood, where most of the mill workers lived. Maria had become quite pretty: pale, slender, with a thick mane of dark hair and wide, clear, sincere eyes. She knew she had been born in the mill where she now worked. They had told her about the death of her unlucky mother, and later, when she asked about her father, she found out that she was the child of an unhappy love affair: her mother had been seduced. They didn't tell her, however, that her boss was the guilty party—the very same boss who still ran the gigantic plant, the man who sometimes stooped down to caress her cheek paternally, yet who felt no remorse when he made her work fourteen-hour shifts.

And so Maria turned twenty years old. She didn't have a boyfriend. The boys she knew, the young male workers who lived in the neighborhood, considered her somewhat like a sister. None of them fell in love with her, as they felt bound by a peaceful friendship rooted in childhood. Maria kept mostly to herself and grew attached to the factory: it seemed to her that its walls, quivering with the vibrations of activity, hid something secret of hers. Sometimes, passing by a certain corridor where the baskets of golden cocoons were piled high to the ceiling, she would feel a strange sense of uneasiness and then flee, looking around her, shivering.

And when she passed by the room where her mother had died while giving birth, she would look at the work station near the *buckets*, the position the poor, young, seduced woman had once occupied, and her kind eyes would mist over with tears.[1]

***

Whether classified as propaganda, social fiction, or anarchist pulp, these sorts of stories serve as useful tools for translating sociopolitical issues into everyday scenarios, in which it is easier to understand the stakes at hand. A technique, perhaps even an art, to stimulate debate and ultimately bring about some sort of change. Bruna Leda Rafanelli (1880–1971) knew this all too well, as the main avenue for her political activism consisted of the creation of an impressive corpus of written work, much of it in the form of fiction propagating anarchist principles: over a few years short of a century, she published fifteen novels, forty-nine short stories, and literally hundreds of articles and essays written between 1900 and the late 1960s. These totals do not take into account a further twenty novels and hundreds of short stories, comic plays, poems, and other essays left unpublished upon her death.

An individualist anarchist, a self-taught intellectual and editor who ran in a variety of radical circles, she was also a *feminilist* and a Muslim. Some of her fellow anarchists considered these identities to be mutually

---

1   Leda Rafanelli, "La figlia della fabbrica" (my translation), in *Bozzetti Sociali*, second edition (Milan: Casa Editrice Sociale, 1921), 115–117. Fondo "Leda Rafanelli-Monanni" [LR-M] conserved at the Archivio Famiglia Berneri-Aurelio Chessa-Reggio Emilia, Biblioteca Panizzi, Reggio-Emilia [ABC]. Note that all translations in this book were performed by the editor. Leda's use of capitalization, italicization, and emphasis are reproduced faithfully in these translations.

exclusive and ultimately contradictory to the general principles of revolutionary libertarianism. This criticism earned Rafanelli a reputation as an eccentric, perhaps even lent her a unique charm, yet due to her editorial prowess and obvious intellect, did little to discredit her.

Rafanelli lived her truth as she saw fit. She refused to conform to the anarchist mainstream, and instead lived her public and private life in strict accordance with her own moral and spiritual code. She was a walking example of individualist anarchism in action. Coming of age at the turn of the century, she worked through one of the most vibrant periods of political and philosophical development in Italy as the country took its first shaky steps as a unified nation. Monarchy, fascism, socialism, theocracy, imperialism, individualism, internationalism: all options were on the table, as nobody could agree upon exactly which political ideology the Italian government should adopt. Amid the roar of voices echoing through the cafes and town squares of the peninsula, those proclaiming anarchist ideas posed the biggest challenges to the dominant political factions, and therefore were the most feared, the most oppressed, and the most creative.

Writers, speakers, and organizers expressed a broad range of interpretations of anarchist principles and practices: among the many approaches, the educationalists believed further education of everyday people was necessary in order to raise awareness as to why revolution was worth the risk. Some insurrectionists, on the other hand, believed the masses were ready as they were to be mobilized into rejecting imposed authority and forcefully reclaiming their own power. This diversity was somewhat responsible for hindering attempts to unify the Italian language branch of the movement under a single definition or objective, and hence precluded any major collective initiative, such as the Paris Commune and Spanish anarchist experiments, although popular insurrections in 1914 and later in 1919–1920 did make it look, momentarily, as if the revolution had finally come to Italy. The ideology of anarchism was expanded to such a variety of applications, and its principles fleshed out in so many different directions that both murderers and pacifists, intellectuals and illiterate farmhands could and did call themselves anarchists. Everyone found their own way to interpret anarchism and, in this way, Rafanelli was no exception.

Leda's *propaganda*—a word that had different connotations, in both Italian and English, during the early 1900s as compared to how we understand it today—made use of a variety of themes and formats. From brief calls to action and short stories illustrating anarchist messages, to longer political novels, essays on the principles of anarchism (particularly free love), coming-of-age stories that served as training manuals for young anarchists, children's stories set in non-European cultures, psychologically astute profiles of the hundreds of men and women she came to know throughout her lifetime: her work was intended not to entertain, but to instruct, to illuminate, to illustrate. Writing for both adults and children, she adjusted her content in order to speak to workers, intellectuals, men, and women, seeking to reach out as far as she could to bring anarchist ideas to the widest possible audience.

This desire culminated in her co-founding two highly influential anarchist publishing houses in Florence and Milan, and she spent forty years of her life working behind the typography machine, organizing new editorial initiatives and churning out her own manuscripts. To our great benefit, her unique story and personality shine through her work, which is often loosely autobiographical and provides a wealth of original ideas and inspiration for modern debates on what it means to be an anarchist, a liberated woman, and a Muslim, or in her case, some version of all three at once. A large amount of her writing is conserved in the Berneri-Aurelio Chessa Family Archives in Reggio Emilia, Italy, which allows us to trace her story as she walked along the margins of society: the fringe often overlooked by the historical record.

***

The boss's son, a young man who had been sent off to school when he was fourteen years old, returned home for good five years later. He was one year younger than Maria. The boss had gotten married right after Rosa's death.

The boy had grown up to be an elegant young man. He was kind, well-mannered, and very friendly. He spent many hours in the factory talking with the workers and seemed to have modern views. He was nice to all of the women, especially the younger women.

One day, however, an older worker grew concerned as she watched *the factory's daughter* and the young boss talking behind a door. They were looking into each other's eyes, and the young maiden had let him take her hand in his...

The woman felt the urgent need to immediately alert her workmates:

"Dear lord! That man is her brother! We forgot to think of this earlier, to warn our daughter...All the girls are fond of that lad and it would be a disaster if he set his sights on Maria...What if they're already in love!? There's no other way around it, we need to tell her immediately."

And the delicate task was given to Sandra, the old woman who the girl lived with.

—

The next morning, on her way to work at a very early hour, *the factory's daughter* looked as if she had aged several years. A heavy pain had spread across her rosy face like a leaden veil. She had a deep wrinkle in the middle of her forehead and her eyes were swollen from a sleepless night of crying.

The previous evening, Sandra had told her the sad truth: the boss was her father! The young man who told her so many sweet and lovely things was *her brother*! He didn't know that either. But she had found out the truth too late, because she was already in love with the young boss!

She mechanically went about her work in the factory that day: her motions were automatic as she went back and forth, pale and silent. Her behavior had changed so drastically that everyone was aware some painful drama was unfolding in the poor young girl's soul. When the other workers asked her what was wrong, she responded with a weak smile:

"Nothing's wrong, *mama*!"

"You look very pale, Maria. Do you want to go home?"

"No, no, I'm just really tired. I'll feel better once I get a good night's sleep."

And all of the workers thought they had done the right thing by telling her the secret. A terrible danger had been avoided.

—

That evening, as the women left the factory and walked home, some of them noticed that Maria was missing. Usually the young girl's nimble silhouette would drift from group to group, greeting all of the workers who had done so much for her.

"She must have already left," some said. "She wasn't feeling well."

But *the factory's daughter* was still there, gasping for breath behind the baskets full of cocoons, her throat slashed by a knife. She laid there alone (in the same exact place where her mother had suffered the embraces of the man who had seduced her), blood pouring out from her neck, with her eyes lost in the shadows of the large, deserted, and silent factory, as the fat yellow cocoons spilled out of their baskets and bathed in the red of her blood.

Meanwhile, the boss sat in his office, telling his son about the marvelous sums of money he had earned with that batch of golden cocoons...[2]

***

Despite such hardline, unambiguous critique of traditional patriarchy and all of its trimmings, one of the more polarizing aspects of Rafanelli's character is her rejection of feminism—a notion she considered to be a product of bourgeois parlors—and her promotion of an ideal that lacks a word in Italian, much less an English translation. *Feminility* is an ad-hoc neologism of femininity and the suffix *-ility*, which refers to the ability and capacity to do something: *feminility* signifies a rejection of patriarchy as well as liberal feminism, while embracing the "natural" order of sexual difference. Accordingly, Leda set out to explore exactly what the essence of womanhood consisted of, beyond its social constructions in an oppressive society: a difficult line of inquiry in a world where women were simply understood as inferior to men.

Whether or not it stands up to queer critique today, *feminility* nevertheless offered an alternative expression of female liberation, without supporting the political structures created under and maintained by a male-dominated system. Furthermore, as an anarchist who considered

---

2   Ibid, 117–119.

the state unnecessary and illegitimate, Leda had no interest in supporting women's right to vote. Instead of advocating inclusion of women in traditional power structures, Rafanelli sought, through her novels featuring female protagonists and her written criticism of liberal feminism, not to mention her own life and intimate relations, to provide a new template for women, so that they could act and live out their authentic selves in lieu of taking up the roles industrial capitalism was creating for them in the image of those it had already created for men.

Equally intriguing, and off-putting, is the idea of an anarchist—who by common definition rejects organized religion—adhering faithfully to the tenets of Islam, especially when the anarchist was born and raised in a country such as Italy, where the influence of the Catholic Church requires no explanation. Perhaps partly a rebellion against other anarchists claiming some form of cultural orthodoxy, Leda's creative interpretation of Islam was nevertheless motivated by a sincere desire to explore spirituality, an inquiry that eventually led her toward mysticism. Islam served as a practical moral code she followed in order to practice a different approach to human relations, thereby challenging the mis-teachings of corrupted European society, while providing a spiritual outlet free from the institutionalized ideology of Catholicism. She pursued her religious studies and reflections largely at home, never proselytizing, and steered clear of joining any Muslim community or place of worship. Hence she customized Islam, perhaps in such a way that more orthodox Muslims might find offensive or even sacrilegious, adding an exotic dimension to her existence and creating the means by which to live out her own unique nature.

Leda walked how she talked, and her life was a testimony to how people can live anarchically free, even within the oppressive society and overbearing institutions of fascism. She flagrantly overturned every externally imposed constraint that came her way. Leda's unique interpretations of such broad philosophical concepts provide us with an opportunity to explore the ideas of women's liberation, Islam, and anarchism outside of the conventions of normal discourse. And although she stayed largely focused on practice by devoting her energy to transmitting the essentials of anarchisms to the general public, her work and example pushed the theoretical limits drawn around these ideologies, sometimes to the amazement, other times to the discomfort, of those around her.

During Leda's time, middle and upper class women were generally limited to one of two professions in Italy: teaching and writing. It was socially acceptable for women to work as teachers, as they would be expected, in their impending motherhood, to be responsible for the domestic education of young people.[3] Writing, as a profession that took place in private, posed little risk to respectability, and work from female authors was expected to be devoted to the moral education of other women, at best, or earnest imitations of men's work or sentimental fluff, at worst.[4] Although the didactic tendency is frequently evident in her output, Leda's work was obviously not geared toward reproducing the morals and values of the dominant social institutions.

However, perhaps because it was so different, or perhaps due to the general stigma attributed to leftist movements and particularly anarchism, Leda's work remained unknown, out-of-print, and untranslated for forty years after her death, save for a collection of letters from her brief friendship with a pre-fascist Benito Mussolini, published in 1946.[5] In 2005, an unpublished manuscript describing her love affair with futurist painter Carlo Carrà was released in a heavily annotated format, followed by a 2007 conference in Reggio Emilia dedicated to exploring her life and ideas, thus rekindling interest in this fascinating figure of the Italian anarchist movement.[6] In 2010, the Italian publisher Nerosubianco Edizioni began publishing collections of her short stories and memoirs, and more scholars have begun including elements of Leda's writings and ideas in recent biographies and academic theses.

Despite all that was lost throughout the decades, an impressive amount of Leda's literary output remains, and in sifting through it we find evidence of a mind that worked in all directions. Her family and friends were a priority in her life, as evidenced by piles of letters exchanged with friends and the many stories for young readers dedicated to her grandchildren. Her pamphlets and essays are naturally provocative, yet her musings on love and eroticism are more subtle and pensive. Her unpublished papers include reactions to current events in international

---

3   Perry Wilson, *Italiane: Biografia del Novecento*, trans. Paola Marangon (Rome-Bari: Edizioni Laterza, 2011), 36–37.

4   Ibid.

5   Leda Rafanelli, *Una Donna e Mussolini* (Milan: Rizzoli, 1946). A first edition was released in 1946 and a second edition was released in 1975, which includes an oft-referenced introduction by Pier Carlo Masini.

6   Alberto Ciampi, ed., *Leda Rafanelli—Carlo Carrà, Un Romanzo: Arte e Politica in un Incontro Ormai Celebre* (Venice: Centro Internazionale della Grafica, 2005).

news, explorations of linguistic structures in Arabic, and memories of fellow anarchists who had since perished or moved to other countries. Some of her novels are clearly instructive, providing new role models in the form of everyday characters who encounter, embrace, and explore ideals of freedom. Other books herald anarchism as an alternative to the injustices of authority, whether political, religious, social, or spiritual, by flagrantly denouncing the violence caused by the imposition of hierarchy. This is how she explains her work in the first pages of *Social Sketches* (*Bozzetti Sociali*), a collection of fifty-six short stories first published in 1910 that includes "The Factory's Daughter":

> In just a few pages, a *social sketch* reflects the sensations experienced and the impressions one receives from the multiform aspects of modern life. Whether wrapped in the fog of an icy, grey, cold evening; sunk in the somber darkness of the slums; lost within the modern-day chasm of a machine shop; or even strolling along the splendid seashore: there are creatures moving about everywhere, human beings who the novelist does not see, who the historian does not recognize, since there is nothing to differentiate them from the masses in which they flounder. They live in houses, in hovels, in the depths of the mines, in the cold solitude of the prisons, in the stillness of the convents, all victims of persecution and pain, all subjected to the orthodoxy of today's laws; even wounded and exasperated rebels, men, women, young adults: people who have been shipwrecked by life, who no one will ever throw a line to. Some of these characters walk through these pages, making brief and realistic appearances in a work we have entitled *Social Sketches*, which also pays tribute to the very famous vignettes written by De Amicis, who situated his wispy plots in the barracks, revealing a wealth of detail and many shades of color in the lives of soldiers. And as the sketches presented in this book reflect the author's ideas, we decided to call them social sketches, although "social" is not the best adjective since it means something very general and lacks a clear and specific definition. Yet, as the people passing through these pages carry the heavy burden of their pain, the light of their hopes and even the quivering stamina of their fate, this work is a form

of sociology studying the oppressed and rebellious nature of these beings. Such a title would generally be given to scientific, economic, or simply literary works when they address or delve into new ideals.

This was just a simple note to explain the book's title.[7]

Rafanelli spent the decades between 1900 and 1930 writing books and pamphlets non-stop, founding and contributing to numerous newspapers, running her own publishing houses, participating in philosophical debates, and rubbing elbows with all of the grandees of radical Italian society; yet due to a series of personal traumas coupled with exhaustion, she withdrew from public life and spent the last forty years of her life making ends meet through working as a fortune teller, staying close to her family, and cultivating her solitude. Her focus slowly shifted from producing politically-charged material to more reflective memoirs, including one major project to reconstruct the history of Italian anarchism during the early twentieth century. Drawing from her personal experiences and commemorating her many acquaintances, she set about to narrate the story of a movement she had personally lived and worked through. Yet this work remained unfinished and unpublished upon her death in 1971.

This book aspires to follow that intention, to tell the fascinating story of Leda's pursuit of freedom from all angles, while providing an outline of the debates and developments in anarchism that surrounded her. The translations presented here represent but a fraction of her total output, falling far short of providing a comprehensive review of her work in its totality: yet perhaps they will inspire the reader's imagination and curiosity to find out more from other sources.

Today, people in "Western" cultures have as many misunderstandings and misconceptions about Muslims as they did, perhaps, during the era of the Crusades. Two generations have come of age since second-wave feminism, and yet a woman's right to choose what to do with her body is still hotly debated. Many of us continue the age-old tradition of questioning the basic institutions of our social reality and wondering whether we can do better. We can only grow wiser from increasing our understanding of different perspectives on feminism, Islam, and anarchism, particularly given the stigma of social and physical violence often and incorrectly attributed to the latter two. Leda's perspective offers a

---

7   Leda Rafanelli, "Introduction," in *Bozzetti Sociali*, 5–6.

convenient vehicle to examine all three dimensions, and her efforts to combine them highlight different facets and compatibilities overlooked when we consider each conviction independently.

This story will be woven together by translations of excerpts of Leda's own work, equal parts fiction, essay, and autobiography. The vast majority of books signed by Leda Rafanelli (or with one of her pseudonyms) never made it intact to library or university collections, and some of what you will read here was never even published: thus this book owes its very existence to the dedicated conservation efforts made by Rafanelli's family and the Archivio Famiglia Berneri-Aurelio Chessa. I would like to extend a special thanks to Fiamma Chessa, curator of the archives, who has been above and beyond generous in sharing her biographical and contextual knowledge in addition to the archive materials.

In the spirit of critical inquiry, and in consideration of the fact that even after a century, Leda Rafanelli's ideas still retain their controversial flavor, the reader is encouraged to question what is presented in these pages. Can religion and anarchism be legitimately synthesized? What about the convergence of pacifism and class struggle, anti-imperialism and internationalism, anti-patriarchy and *feminility*? Despite the un-wavering stance taken towards such issues in forthright propaganda, any writer worth her salt would prefer her work to stimulate discussion, rather than be swallowed down, unquestioned, and accepted without debate.

***

The springtime sunshine burst through the wide-open win-dows of the classroom in the old schoolhouse, followed by the fragrances from the little garden adjacent to the building. The May roses were already in full bloom. And that bright, intense light cheerfully illuminated the merry group of young pupils: about fifty children, all younger than ten years old.

The teacher walked into the room. Still in the early years of adulthood, she was beautiful in a serious and earnest way. She had a delicate profile, wide eyes flecked with green glints, and a small, supple mouth. A precociously grey mane of hair seemed out of place on top of her young head, and left people guessing how old she might be. Her students loved her how she was, youthful in her gestures, in her glances, in her smiles, just like their older sisters: and grey on top, just like their grandmothers. And she loved the children, too. As soon as she entered the room, the noisy group greeted her with a kind: "Good morning, Mrs. Teacher." When she responded, her clear voice took on an almost maternal tenderness: "Good morning, my dears."

Her gentle hands caressed two little heads in front of her, and she soon became aware that a girl's pale face appeared to be stricken with pain. She bent down, bringing her fresh cheek near the little forehead burning with fever. She called the custodian to accompany the little girl home.

"She has a fever, let's hope it's nothing serious. Tell her mother to keep her warm and put her to bed."

Then she asked the little one: "Did you feel sick this morning at home?"

"No, but I was coughing last night…"

"Go home, honey. Stay in bed like a good girl. I'll come by to check on you later tonight."

She knew how to make them love her! Even when she was strict. As soon as the sick child left, the teacher noticed that one of the older students, Ninetto, was eating. He had taken advantage of the few minutes his teacher was distracted to scarf down huge chunks of his bread.

"We do not eat in class, Ninetto!"

The intonation of her voice was harsh. But none of her students were afraid of that *stern voice*. Her kind eyes sparkled with laughter as they gazed upon that handsome, ravenous boy—so healthy and robust, so exuberant with life, sitting there and unable to keep still!

The teacher sat down. The boys and girls found their seats as if they were purposefully trying to make as much noise as possible. The large room was blazing with sun and the teacher went to close the canvas curtains. On the white wall, between the map of Italy and the portrait of the king, there was a large black crucifix: this insignia of martyrdom was the only gloomy note in the village's old schoolhouse.

She began the lesson.

As had been the custom for years in that school, which remained tied to the same old *method* used generation after gencration, the teacher first led her students in reciting a prayer. Then, for the older children, she read a little story that they would have to rewrite from memory: *Resignation is the greatest virtue.* That was the title.

The morning passed calmly. The teacher read and explained a chapter of religious history: it was no small struggle to explain the complex will of the Lord, who commanded one of his devotees to sacrifice his son's life as proof of his devotion. This didn't make a lot of sense in the minds of her young pupils. Then it was time for her students to read. She opened the reader to a random page, announced the page number and had one of the children stand up and read. The young boy's fresh voice pronounced in a monotone drone:

"*The duties of a good citizen.*"

He continued reading for a few pages, and finally enunciated—this time with feeling—the *moral* of the story: *Love your king, serve your country.*

"Bravo! A perfect ten!" approved the teacher, as the child sat down, satisfied. Not everyone got a good *grade* in reading!

The teacher went on with the lesson. And yet she didn't have the slightest idea that she was using all of her passion, all of her love, to inject poison into these young souls.

Didn't she realize she was preparing *her* children for a life of slavery and pain?

"Resign yourselves!" she told them. But did she think about the many injustices that strong, knowledgeable adults naturally want to rebel against?

Her *lesson* taught them to fully devote their energy to slavery and lies. She wanted the poor to work without complaining; she believed that the rich could, through *charity*, relieve the miseries that God allowed. *God's will!* Her moral education was based on God's will!

"Love your *king*, serve your country. Do your *duty*. Respect *authority*. Resign yourself to adversity and have faith in *God*."

God, king, country, authority! These were the masters that she herself dogmatically drilled into the oblivious souls of her children. *Resignation, duty!* These were the *virtues* she taught them to practice.

Poor teacher, so beautiful, sweet and good! She was more ignorant than her pupils. She ignored life and was unable to fight for anything. She believed in all of the inequalities, she kneeled down in front of all of the idols, she lived in the past and for the past. She preferred—without even giving it a second thought—evil over good, lies over truth, cruelty over righteousness, weak cowardice over rebellious strength. And she breathed life into these ideas, and thus poisoned her young virgin souls.

The sun and the fragrances from the garden filtered through the large room of the old schoolhouse. Nature smiled. And none of the parents of these children ever thought about the poison that was seeping into the minds of their little children with every word they heard. None of them ever thought that in years to come, these future men and women would desperately search for truth and light amidst the thick darkness that had swallowed them![8]

---

8   Leda Rafanelli, "Il veleno," *Bozzetti Sociali*, 335–338.

CHAPTER II
Printing Presses and Papyrus

In my subconscious Being—still enshrouded in the clouds of my early years that, due to challenging family trials, proved to be rather "difficult"—a violent, confused love for Life exploded, with the desire—the need, I would say—to use my life for "something." Something that I could not yet define, that I could not yet understand, that I could not yet fit into my everyday existence. It was a secret impulse toward an Ideal that I could not yet translate into action, insomuch as it was still wrapped in the clouds of ignorance, but already strong and living through the reality of my Instinct. A healthy instinct, a rebellious instinct that yearned for a different type of life than that which passed by every day, an instinct which asked to be freed from the darkness that still enveloped me. A deep, aching sense of "nostalgia" lived inside of me, the same sentiment that had already pushed my only brother to enlist as a cabin boy on a dingy Sailing ship, with the sole objective of reaching the East he so longed for, where he thought he could live a free and primitive life. And this nostalgia—which he only understood and realized over time—also consumed me and prevented me from living "in the present." It made me an outsider, scornful of everything that comprised, unfortunately, the reality of my adolescence, from which I wanted to escape.[1]

---

1   Leda Rafanelli, *Gli Ultimi Internazionalisti,* unpublished manuscript, date unknown, 1–2. Fondo "LR-M" conserved at the ABC.

***

Leda, as she was known to her parents, friends, and grandchildren alike, was born in 1880 in Pistoia, a city in the heart of Tuscany. Her mother, Elettra Gaetani, was the daughter of blue-collar workers and grew up in poverty, while Leda's father, Augusto Rafanelli, came from a well-off middle class family.

Despite what Leda writes in the loosely autobiographical sketch above from *The Last Internationalists,* her brother Metello Brunone (1883–1969) was not a sailor, though he often depicted the sea in his paintings and even wrote a book about Italian sailors in Tripoli (*Marinai italini a Tripoli*), published in 1913. Primarily a visual artist, he also wrote adventure stories and translated a few P.G. Wodehouse books for his sister's publishing house in the 1930s. He and Leda coauthored their first book in 1897, published by the Giuseppe Flori print shop: *Thoughts* (*Pensieri*) is a short collection of a few dozen poems, generally three to five stanzas long, on subjects ranging from the Tuscan countryside to a piece of candy. Simple, honest, and playful, the work represents a promising beginning for two young, artistic souls.

The Rafanelli family was evidently open-minded and supportive of creative endeavors, not to mention modestly well-off, at least initially. Although photography was still a novelty in the late nineteenth century, a collection of portraits document the growth of the two siblings from their earliest years. Sometimes they're shown standing calmly in nice clothes and good shoes, other times a teenage Leda is seen wearing necklaces around her forehead or covering her décolletage with ivy and chard. Leda would continue the habit of sitting for portraits throughout her life, right up to the last series of photos taken in 1971: in her nineties, she still drew lines of kohl around her eyes and wore gigantic hoops dangling from her ears, posing with a large, stuffed snake coiled around her neck as she gazes brazenly at the camera.

Leda's memoirs recount her father's initial resistance to his daughter's budding interest in anarchism, fed by the influences she came into contact with when she first started working at a print shop in the 1890s. Mr. Rafanelli feared the anarchist movement was some form of secret society that would put his daughter's life in danger; furthermore, he didn't see any reason for her to be so interested in what he called "political" affairs, as such matters were clearly "things that women are unable to understand."[2] Her rebellious instinct and eagerness to go against what was considered right and normal in a lawful society initially made no sense to her parents, who wanted nothing more than a healthy and peaceful existence for their children.

However, Leda actually refers to her mother as her first convert, stating that Mrs. Rafanelli was the first person who, after listening to her daughter explain current social issues and the mechanisms of state oppression, decided that she, too, would join the struggle against oppressive systems of authority. She did, however, beg her daughter to call herself a *socialist*, rather than an *anarchist*, since *anarchist* was a scary word and *socialist* sounded much nicer.[3] Leda's parents eventually grew to embrace her philosophical convictions and unconventional lifestyle, and she counted upon their support throughout many decades of activism and subversive publishing.

Particularly interesting is Leda's analysis of Mrs. Rafanelli's spiritual practice, which may very well have helped her daughter make a preliminary distinction between religion and spirituality:

> My mother is a believer, but a non-practicing one, and even as a believer she is rather open-minded and anti-dogmatic. She thinks that God—meaning some type of higher Power or Force that we do not understand—exists, but has absolutely nothing to do with trivial affairs or the petty problems of human beings. She prays to God out of her instinctive atavism—without feeling the need to go and look for God in a Church—to her, prayer is merely a way to invoke Health or Life on our behalf. She certainly doesn't pray the way those extremely religious little old ladies pray—like one we met the first time we went to Florence, who would ask God for the Lotto numbers.
>
> My mother also venerates Mary, the holy mother, but she venerates her for being a Woman who suffered because of how much she loved her Son, a Prophet of God, not the Son of God. And she left us free to think with our own brains, as she

2   Leda Rafanelli, *La Grande Maestra*, unpublished manuscript, date unknown, 57. Conserved in a private collection owned and kindly made available by Fiamma Chessa.
3   Ibid., 51–52.

had faith in our goodness and virtue, since she understands
the laws of human love better than the laws of divine love.
And maybe that's why it was so easy for us to get along.[4]

After enjoying what sounds like a fun, stimulating, and secure childhood, Leda was drastically affected by some sort of misfortune that befell
the Rafanelli household in the 1890s. Both the historical record and Leda's own memoirs remain mute on the details, yet the prevalent rumor is
that her father was sentenced to a few years in prison for nonpolitical reasons. Whatever the exact nature of these "challenging family trials," they
compelled her to leave school and start working at a print shop. Thus,
with nothing more than an elementary school education, Leda officially
joined the ranks of the working class as an adolescent, learning the trade
and techniques of the printing press.

She was first hired at a print shop near Piazza San Bartolomeo in
downtown Pistoia. Day in and day out, she would stand at the machines
and read pages and pages of new material, absorbing the information
being conveyed in a variety of subjects and languages, as well as the text's
vocabulary, grammar, and syntax as she laid out each word, letter by letter, on the typesetting machine. Not only did her work in the print shop
allow her to continue her education in a noninstitutionalized manner,
it also brought her into close, personal contact with activists and their
work, as she described later in an unpublished essay:

> Among the people who worked at the little local print shop,
> one boy stood out from all the rest. Aside from two or three
> older employees, who got a lot done but didn't talk much, the
> young workers were rather carefree, lazy, full of things to say
> and low on morals. Alfredo, however, wasn't from Livorno: he
> was from Prato, the city that became famous for the murder
> of the king during the early years of the new century.
>   Everyone felt dissatisfied and uncomfortable in that
> wretched, cramped environment, where workers were
> burdened with exhausting work and abysmally low pay. In
> the full bloom of youth, their happy years slipped away in a
> haze of incomprehension and fatigue, and those who had a
> free spirit and a superior mentality yearned for a better life,

---

4   Ibid., 53.

wondering why they had been stricken with such an inexplicably unjust fate. They felt discouraged. The new century had not brought new light to the proletariat, who were still too afraid and ignorant. Sporadic revolts led by oppressed and indecisive beings with a cloudy awareness of their own principles, who had convinced themselves that they could solve complex problems by setting fire to a few tax offices, made it harder for propagandists to spread new Ideas. People knew, of course, that Socialism opened a path towards enlightenment in the midst of so many shadows, but few had the strength or courage to head off in that direction.

We would print copies of a socialist journal in our shop, and even if there was no profit involved, our boss never told them no. However, instead of having the workers do it, he would compose the proof himself, and the shop leader would handle the page setting. They printed it on their own during the evening, and not a single scrap copy or draft could ever be found. We would buy a copy whenever we had a little extra money, but it was often hard to find. They only printed a few copies, and many times they were sequestered.

One April morning, as we all came in to start work at the Shop, Alfredo took me aside. He was not associated with any one group in particular, but he had given me a few pamphlets to read and it seemed as if we shared some of the same ideas. Apart from the others, he handed me a folded sheet of paper and, getting straight to the point, told me:

"Listen…while everyone's on break, I need you to compose this in legal format using font 12. Don't do a proof beforehand, and pass it on to Gherardo when you're done. And don't say a word about it to anyone."

I agreed with a nod and slipped the paper under my blouse, as if it were a love letter. I was very young and enthusiastic, and at the print shop they considered me one of the boys. I was overjoyed that Alfredo had put his trust in me, and during our break, while some workers ate their lunches and others stayed behind to clean up, I quickly composed what was written on that paper while reading it through: it was propaganda, a call for action on May first.

I was incredibly proud. I felt my self-confidence had grown considerably.

I printed out the lines and put them in a folder together with the manuscript, then noticed Gherardo was in the room. A poor, frail boy, he was nevertheless very skilled with the machines. He passed by with a seemingly indifferent attitude, yet his eyes lit up when I handed him the packet. We all knew that he was very unhappy: his family mistreated him and his father even beat him. But he, too, was proud to be a part of this secret.

We felt that we had done something that was forbidden, yet pure.

I never found out how Alfredo and that boy managed to print copies of those little bills. Often, during our breaks, the other workers would print their own business cards or advertising leaflets, and I assume Alfredo was good at hiding these sorts of things. Three days later, he gave me one of "our" little manifestos, and I was delighted.[5]

In 1861, 72 percent of men and 84 percent of women in Italy were illiterate.[6] After the institution of compulsory education with the 1859 Casati law, these numbers slowly decreased by about five to ten percent per decade: by 1901, only 42.5 percent of men and 54.4 percent of women were illiterate.[7] As literacy rates rose, access to the printing press represented a new tool for those looking to influence popular opinion. Print shops, therefore, played a crucial role in promoting the ideas that went against the established order—ideas that often would not be accepted for publication in a mainstream newspaper—and many print shops in Italy were owned by people who supported or at least sympathized with radical ideas, thus becoming critical resources for fin-de-siècle anarchist groups and initiatives.

One of the cheapest and most immediate ways to diffuse subversive ideas was through pamphlets. In their simplest form, pamphlets appear

5   Leda Rafanelli, *Solidarietà*, unpublished manuscript, date unknown, 1–2. Fondo "LR-M" conserved at the ABC.

6   Perry Wilson, *Italiane: Biografia del Novecento*, trans. Paola Marangon (Rome-Bari: Edizioni Laterza, 2011), 24.

7   Ibid.

as booklets with eight pages created from folding a sheet of paper in half lengthwise and then widthwise, providing just enough space for a 250 or 300 word commentary or denunciation, a short essay, or a quick social sketch. Either distributed for free or at the bargain price of one cent, pamphlets were, alongside the larger format newspapers that proliferated during the first decades of the twentieth century, essential tools in strengthening the growing trend of associationism (organizing into independent, non-governmental, and non-church groups) among blue-collar workers.

Historically, in Italy and elsewhere, anarchists have largely acted upon the conviction that an individual's social and economic emancipation can only be achieved through raising their moral and political awareness, whether by reading libertarian materials or listening to talented orators. Absorbing the materials that came through the print shop, Leda came to understand the issues behind the major political and ideological debates underway and, as a teenager, sympathized with the anarchists, who also bore the "outsider" identity she herself had identified with very early in life.

She took to producing her own work early on: after co-authoring *Thoughts* in her early teens, she started contributing short pieces to leftist publications. Given the variety of pen names she used and the plethora of newspapers, journals, and magazines that cropped up every year around the turn of the century—often for only a few issues—we have no idea how many articles, stories, and poems she wrote over her lifetime. However, judging from the clippings she kept, the number is somewhere in the hundreds.

In her memoirs written over half a century later, she describes how she sent a poem entitled *We Are Hawsers* (*Noi siamo gomene;* "hawsers" are thick ropes used for anchoring or towing ships), to the official journal of the socialist party. It was approved for publication by Filippo Turati (1857–1932), one of the members who founded the Italian socialist party in 1892. Turati was a poet himself, famous for penning the lyrics of the Workers' Hymn (*Inno dei Lavoratori*), a song used to inspire and unite workers during strikes and demonstrations. Turati's encouragement and praise of Leda's talent no doubt inspired her to continue pursuing both the craft of political writing and her commitment to radical ideas:

> I wrote this simple poem when I was a young girl, just a poor worker at a print shop. In those days, it was dangerous to call yourself a socialist or a libertarian. I had developed a sincere

friendship with an anarchist from Prato (Bresci had already committed his regicide) and after several years I wrote about it in an autobiographical article.[8] But sometime during the dark beginning of the new century, I sent these verses, transcribed onto a card decorated with a red carnation, to Filippo Turati, the great socialist, who remained loyal to his ideals until his death. At that time, he was the only one I had heard of.

WE ARE HAWSERS

Individual threads of blonde hemp
are so light, invisible, intangible—
you hold one between your fingers without noticing it,
you throw it to the wind, and it takes to flight.

But many threads of blonde hemp,
all united, tied tightly together,
form incredibly strong ropes,
oblivious to the wind that bears down upon them
in the middle of the Sea, on ships full of cargo,
strong, superbly resistant—

This is the strength of the enslaved people,
this is the great power of unity!
Compagni! We, divided, are the weak
light threads of the blonde plant,
together, the incredibly robust hawsers,
that hold ships together amid the waves!

To those who work, we say: UNITE!
You have the power in your hands!
WORKERS! THE COVETED VICTORY OF
    TOMORROW
CAN BE YOURS!

---

8   Gaetano Bresci, a native of Prato, killed King Umberto I on July 29, 1900: this would actually occur a few years after Leda claimed to have written and submitted this poem. Time inconsistencies are frequently found in her memoirs, which she mostly wrote in her seventies and eighties.

Turati wrote back to me: "Dear *Compagna*, this Poem can be published in one of our propaganda newspapers." That made me happy.[9]

***

Fin-de-siècle Italy was boiling over with innovative, progressive, and reactionary perspectives on how society should be organized. Many of these perspectives challenged the legitimacy of the newly founded national government, a constitutional monarchy that largely excluded people who did not own property from political participation. Civil disobedience, strikes, street fights, and general insurrection had fanned the flames of the *risorgimento*, the great resurgence of national sentiment that eventually resulted in the unification of the Kingdom of Italy, a movement led by Giuseppe Garibaldi (1807–1882) and Camillo Cavour (1810–1861) in the 1850s and 1860s. However, especially in light of the political and economic disparities between Northern and Southern Italy, many people were not pleased with the new king Vittorio Emanuele II (1820–1878), and used the same tools of resistance and revolt to re-assert local autonomy or to advocate for another political system entirely.

The nascent Italian nation was founded on a peninsula accustomed to centuries of power struggles between the imperial Catholic church and feudal city-states: centralized government was a relatively new and untested tactic. From 1861–1900 alone, the government was led by no less than sixteen prime ministers, oscillating between fairly liberal and harshly conservative, during a total of twenty-two terms. To add fuel to the fire, the late yet cataclysmic arrival of the industrial revolution in the north and crippling rural poverty in the south inspired massive waves of internal and external migration. People were moving around, bumping up against one another, exchanging ideas, and forming bonds of solidarity in order to address a variety of common concerns. Marxists, anarchists, and socialists, although not the only voices participating in public debate, were all collectively referred to as radicals since they advocated an entire revision of the political system. By means of contrast, the strategy of working within the current political system was advocated

---

9   Leda Rafanelli, *Noi siamo gomene*, transcription with notes, date unknown. Fondo "Leda Rafanelli-Marina Monanni-Maria Laura Filadri" ["LR-MM-MLF"] conserved at the ABC.

by Republican supporters of Mazzini, masons, and early trade unionists. Thus the radicals rallied in piazzas and cafes, publishing profusely, organizing lectures, demonstrations, and revolts in hopes of transforming, or even erasing, the newly-formed nation, replacing it with a society focused on the well-being of the proletariat masses, rather than the elite minority.

As evidenced by the number of prime ministers coming in and out of office over so few years, those in charge of running the government were unable to agree upon a common political and cultural platform. Without charismatic, consistent leadership to explain the changes taking place, national economic reforms met with indifference or anti-institutional resistance, which delayed the development of a shared feeling of belonging to a national community. The state was often decried as an illegitimate and unnatural phenomenon, countered by growing associationism among its population, as well as the gradual formation of a working class. The lack of solidarity between agricultural workers of the rural working class and industrial workers of the urban working class may very well have been the decisive factor that saved the nascent government from being overthrown.

The new government did have its successes, including the creation of national infrastructure and the gradual extension of voting and other rights to the general male population. Yet the masses were still more likely to worry about famine and pestilence than complain about not being able to cast a ballot, and the national government's failure to provide timely assistance opened the space even wider for radical groups.

Anarchists generally distinguished themselves from other ideological groups due to their essential belief in the illegitimacy of institutionalized authority—whether emanating from the church, the state, or the social elite—and its abolition via the dissolution of power. This conflicted directly with socialist objectives, which advocated for the seizure of power by the people, who would then transform the state into a socialist government. Anarchists believed this would merely result in trading in one political hierarchy for another, and would not end up changing anything but the details in the long run. Yet, in practice, this division can be deceptive, particularly when considering how terms such as libertarian socialism or anarcho-communism are used[10]; the boundaries between these ideologies have never been impermeable, and collaborations across them more frequent than commonly assumed. Leda contributed

10   The same applies to the Italian language, in which terms such as *anarcosocialismo* and *anarco-comunismo* are used.

her anarchist articles to socialist and syndicalist newspapers and retained lifelong friendships with activists from all camps. Her teenage adherence to anarchism over socialism was explained in her own words: "*Well*, I thought, logically, *being an Anarchist means something more than being a Socialist*. And I felt that I was an Anarchist, not just for love of Freedom, but because it was a more extreme faith."[11]

In fact, the creation of anarchist dogma providing precise definitions for the principles of anarchism, would be considered anti-anarchist by many: anarchism could be better conceived as a movement, not a political party. Hence a variety of anarchisms flourished, expressed through propagandists, who generally took up the task of preparing the masses intellectually for the revolution, and insurrectionists, who sought to coax change along through disruptive and subversive activities. In reality, the most prominent anarchists—such as a young Andrea Costa, Carlo Caffiero and Errico Malatesta—were more likely to employ a mixture of insurrection and propaganda, depending on the task at hand.

In 1898, Francesco Saverio Nitti, who would serve a brief term as Italy's prime minister in 1919, published an article titled *Italian Anarchists* in the North American Review explaining, to his international audience, that: "Anarchists are rebels; and, in all time, among rebels some have been generous, some violent, some perverse. There are idealist anarchists and criminal ones; the evil is that the latter are generally the most conspicuous."[12] His article intended to answer the question why anarchists— and Italian anarchists, at that—were responsible for the recent deaths of so many heads of state: the president of the French Third Republic Sadi Carnot (1894), Empress Elisabeth of Austria (1898), and Spanish Prime Minister Antonio Cánovas del Castillo (1897) were killed by Sante Geronimo Caserio, Luigi Lucheni, and Michele Angiolillo, respectively, who were all, incidentally, Italian anarchists.

Nitti attributes this correlation not to anarchist principles, but to the long-standing cultural value throughout the Italian peninsula of making heroes out of men who murder powerful rulers: "Caserio, Angiolillo, Luccheni [sic] follow without intending to do so, perhaps without knowing that they do so, the tradition of Agesilao Milano, Orsini, and of the numberless conspirators and regicides whom the middle classes in

---

11   Leda Rafanelli, *La Grande Maestra*, 34.

12   Francesco Nitti, "Italian Anarchists," *The North American Review* Vol. 167 No. 504 (1898), 598–608.

Italy have glorified. The radical bourgeoisie of Italy has elevated, in other times, the murder of a tyrant into an act of heroism. There are streets that are named from regicides, and towns that pride themselves upon having given birth to them. [...] We must add that in the schools of Italy, an error never too much to be deplored, they make an apology for regicide. Unlearned teachers do not explain the difference between martyr and murderer. The history of ancient Rome is full of murders of tyrants or aspirants to tyranny. An individual becomes thus the avenger and the deliverer of society."[13]

On the other side of the spectrum from these few high-profile assassinations, insurrectional Italian anarchists dedicated themselves to organizing popular mobilizations in order to overthrow authority at a local, grassroots level. During the 1877 insurrection in the Matese mountains, for example, a small band of anarchists entered the town hall of the village of Letino, burned official government documents and spoke to the villagers, in the local dialect, about what a social revolution could do for them. The local priest, Don Raffaele Fortini, got into the spirit and gave a speech on the similarities between socialism[14] and the Gospels, declaring that the band of radicals were "true apostles sent by the Lord to preach his divine laws."[15] With the father's blessing, the band went on to occupy the neighboring village, Gallo, and continue drumming up resistance against the King's rule. A few days later, twelve thousand troops had surrounded the area and shots were exchanged, leading to the death of one of the troops and the injury of a second. Authorities diffused the news of this violent ending in order to justify arguments to repress the circulation of socialist ideas and adopt a more authoritarian approach to managing social dissidence.

In 1878, the Church issued the Quod Apostolici Muneris, an overtly anti-socialist, anti-communist, and anti-nihilist encyclical signed by Pope Leo XIII, interpreted, by leftist critics, as a sign of a pact with the Italian government to go on a witch hunt. Demonizing those who challenged the social order as "the deadly plague that is creeping into the very fibers of human society," this circular was used as moral justification to

---

13   Ibid.
14   Here, socialism refers to collective ownership of social goods and cooperative management of the same, not the socialist movement.
15   Pier Carlo Masini, *Storia degli anarchici italiani da Bakunin a Malatesta (1862–1892)* (Milan: Rizzoli: 1969), 121.

persecute, harass, and shut down subversives: "We speak of that sect of men who, under various and almost barbarous names, are called socialists, communists, or nihilists, and who, spread over all the world, and bound together by the closest ties in a wicked confederacy, no longer seek the shelter of secret meetings, but, openly and boldly marching forth in the light of day, strive to bring to a head what they have long been planning—the overthrow of all civil society whatsoever."[16] The church was not opposed to helping the poor, yet it was very much in favor of maintaining the social hierarchy that created poverty, and thus lumped antihierarchicals into the category of heretic. A decade and a half later, right after the 1894 assassination of Sadi Carnot, Prime Minister Francesco Crispi (1819–1901) passed three laws in Italy: the first outlawing possession of explosives, the second restricting freedom of the press especially as regards the publication of inflammatory material, and the third prohibiting associations and meetings of people who intended to subvert the social order, while also establishing penal colonies especially for subversives.[17]

In terms of the actual "threat" posed by anarchists, however, Nitti noted, in the same article published in 1898: "How many anarchists are there in Italy? It is impossible to give any answer to this question. A person who occupied a high political office and whose duty it was to follow the reports periodically sent to the government, told me that there are in Italy no more than three or four thousand active anarchists. But this number may be very far from the truth."[18]

What we do know for sure is that many anarchists in Italy wrote, published, and otherwise found a way to make their names known to their contemporaries and to history. The Russian anarchist Mikhail Bakunin (1814–1876) is widely credited as a founder of collectivist anarchism as well as the person who introduced the anarchist movement to Italy during the 1860s, right after the unification of the kingdom of Italy. Bakunin gradually developed a plan for a decentralized Europe, abolishing the nation state and allowing for the proliferation of federated

---

16   Quod Apostolici Muneris, (Libreria Editrice Vaticana, 1878). URL: http://www.vatican.va/holy_father/leo_xiii/encyclicals/documents/ hf_l-xiii_enc_28121878_quod-apostolici-muneris_en.html.

17   Alessandro Aruffo, *Gli Anarchici Italiani 1870–1970*, (Rome: Datanews, 2010), 75.

18   Nitti, *Italian Anarchists*, Vol. 167.

collectivities. One of his protégés, Errico Malatesta (1853–1932), remembering his impressions the first time he met Bakunin, wrote: "Bakunin had come to shake up all traditions, all social, political, patriotic dogmas, which the masses of Neapolitan *intellectuals* had considered, up until that point, to be firm and indisputable truths. For some, Bakunin was the barbarian from the North, a Godless man without a Homeland, without any respect for anything sacred, who posed a threat to holy Latin and Italian civilization. For others, he was the man who had brought a breath of fresh air to the dead pond of Neapolitan traditions, who had opened the eyes of the youth, whom he had introduced to new, wider horizons: these were Fanelli, De Luca, Gambuzzi, Tucci, Paladino, etc., the first socialists, the first internationalists, the first anarchists of Naples and Italy."[19]

Bakunin directly inspired Carlo Cafiero (1846–1892) to further elaborate the theory and practice of anarcho-communism, which essentially postulated that there could be no freedom without anarchism and no equality without communism (meaning, the re-appropriation of all resources and land, not the Marxist doctrine of communism). The aforementioned Errico Malatesta would go on to be one of the most prolific advocates of anarcho-communism, involved in dozens of strikes, insurrections, and demonstrations, and one of his fellow organizers, Andrea Costa (1851–1910), eventually left the anarchist movement to co-found Italian socialism.

These are but a few of the names of anarchists who might have been counted among the "three or four thousand" active in Italy at the turn of the century. But how did a young Italian woman with anarchist leanings come into contact with Islam? It's assumed that Leda was first introduced to the Muslim world when she spent three or four months in Egypt around 1900, a trip she perhaps allegedly took in order to avoid the fallout from a family disgrace, such as her father's imprisonment, if he was indeed incarcerated for a few years.[20] Leda wrote prolifically about her time in the "land of the Pharaohs" in several different autobiographical works, though she glosses over the specific details of the trip, including how she got to North Africa, precisely who she stayed with, and why she only spent a few months there. To date, research into public records has

19 Pier Carlo Masini, *Storia degli anarchici italiani da Bakunin a Malatesta (1862–1892)*, 28–29.
20 Pier Carlo Masini, Introduction to Rafanelli, Leda *Una Donna e Mussolini*, 8.

not provided any information on issuance of a passport or other travel documents to Leda, and it seems odd that a young woman would have taken such a trip by herself, assuming she went unaccompanied. The full story remains a mystery.

With a history spanning thousands of years and all of its incredible relics from ancient times, Egypt has long captured the imagination of intellectuals and travelers. Before 1800, Egypt was closed off to European powers, who had already developed a taste for exploration and colonization in other areas of the African continent. Well beyond the age of the pharaohs, nineteenth-century Egypt was technically under the control of the Ottoman Empire, which granted the region the status of a semi-autonomous province, given the fact that it was rather difficult to control.

In the 1850s, the Ottoman Empire struck a deal with interested European parties that led to the construction of the Suez canal, which took a decade to dig. Through the 1870s, thousands of Italians, mostly from the Tuscany region where Leda grew up, were recruited to help with the construction. A large number of them settled down and stayed in Egypt, opening their own businesses and raising their families. Many Italians originally based in Egypt would go on to wield significant political and cultural influence in the twentieth century, including the founder of futurism, Filippo Tommaso Marinetti, and the modernist writer Giuseppe Ungaretti. The Italian community in Cairo numbered 18,575 by 1927; but even more lived in Alexandria, which boasted a population of 24,280 Italian expats in that same year.[21] As was the case in other countries with large populations of Italian immigrants, new communities were formed reflecting their regional roots—for example, a Venetian neighborhood was formed in Cairo—although other Italians integrated into Egyptian society, adopting local customs and learning the language.

The first waves of Italian immigrants were originally attracted to Egypt by the lucrative jobs available in building the canal. Yet through the fascist era, North Africa became a refuge for those seeking to escape state persecution. Ironically enough, the large Italian expat community in Egypt was full of people who were sympathetic to the anticolonial movement. Pier Carlo Masini, an Italian historian who specialized in anarchist history, deemed that "The Italian language anarchist movement in Egypt was one of the oldest and most robust branches of the movement,"

---

21   Marta Petricioli, *Oltre il Mito: L'Egitto degli italiani (1917–1947)*, (Milan, Bruno Mandadori, 2007), 7.

due to the number of working class laborers who moved there as well as the intellectuals and activists who traveled through.[22]

The Bulacco print shop in Cairo, the first printer in Egypt to compose with Arabic characters, was set up after the Egyptian government sent a delegation to Milan to learn printing techniques. Numerous radical publications came out of Alexandria, including the first Italian language internationalist newspaper printed abroad in 1877, *The Worker* (*Il Lavoratore*).

The word *internationalist* was originally used to refer to members of the International Workingmen's Association, also called the First International, which was a pan-European organization created in 1864 to unite various left-wing movements, including anarchist, socialist, Marxist, and syndicalist groups and activists. The idea was to work in solidarity, beyond the borders imposed by nation states, in order to overthrow the oppressive ruling class and their abusive practice of capitalism. The First International was divided and soon dissolved after the schism of 1872, when Bakunin accused Karl Marx of being an authoritarian and declared that any future Marxist government would be just as tyrannical as the people they were trying to replace. This drew a deep line between anarchism and socialism, as whatever form of organization or collectivism anarchism promoted, it was bound to follow an anti-authoritarian, federalized logic in direct contrast to the centralized, authoritarian program of socialism or communism.

Further revivals of the international (the Second International, the Third International, etc.) would be formed throughout the coming decades, yet these were socialist or communist associations that excluded the anarchist movement, which formed its own, generally short-lived, international associations as well (the St. Imier International and further reincarnations of the International Workers'/Working People's Associations). Therefore, someone who identified as an "internationalist" could be a socialist or an anarchist or a communist: the common denominator is that he or she belonged to an association that acknowledged the global dimension of the revolutionary struggle, and sought solidarity with other, like-minded activists and organizers across the confines of national borders. Although not all internationalists were anarchists, internationalism was fundamentally a condition of being an

---

22   Pier Carlo Masini, Introduction to Rafanelli, Leda, *Una Donna e Mussolini*, 7–8.

anarchist, as someone who did not recognize national borders drawn up by governments as legitimate.

In addition to its internationalist Italian radicals, Egypt had its own opposition movements brewing. Reactionary activity heated up in 1879, led by Egyptian nationalist Colonel Ahmed Urabi and fueled by widespread opposition to the Egyptian government's collusion with foreign powers. Eventually suppressed in 1882 with a British invasion and bombardment, anticolonial sentiment nevertheless remained boiling for several decades until the 1919 revolution, which culminated in Egypt's independence from British control in 1922.

Urban Egypt had, therefore, many of the same influences Leda came into contact with as a teenager working at a print shop in Pistoia. She describes, in her memoirs, a particularly decisive encounter in Alexandria:

> One day, a long time ago, a girl—still an adolescent, really—wandered through the back alleys of Iskanderiyah, curious and excited. She had made all kinds of sacrifices and surmounted a variety of obstacles in order to come to this city and stay with the family of friends from Livorno. She had come for a purpose all her own, following her own dream, under the illusion that she could learn the Arabic language in such a short time, which was only proof of her naïve ignorance. Her host family had lived in Egypt for over twenty years but spoke little Arabic. They peppered their conversation with just a few Arabic words related to their business dealings (importing and selling Italian products) whenever they spoke to their helpers and servants, who were also Italian. The young woman understood that, even if she spent a year with that friendly family, she would never speak Arabic. But if she went another route, she would be able to master the language.
>
> She had to leave *her* beloved Egypt in just a few days. She had seen the Great Pyramids and the mysterious Sphinx. She felt magnetized to that marvelous land—especially Cairo, a city called the "mother of the World" in Arabic. She felt as if she had lived those days in her true homeland, the homeland she chose to belong to, a land that resonated deeply among those who felt and explored its secret roots.

She bid a silent farewell to the city where she had come
ashore. But would the memory of Cairo remain only in her
heart? *Will I come back here when I'm older?* she wondered. She
had heard people say that "whoever drinks the water of the
Nile will return again."

Trying to imprint every image she saw into her memory,
she slowly ambled through a nearly deserted neighborhood
of squat houses that had no doors, shacks whose windows
were blocked by iron bars. Suddenly she noticed a tiny little
shop. The small store window was full of papers, spread out
and covered with cancelled stamps, alongside collectibles and
prints showing famous Italian landmarks: Naples crowned
by Vesuvius, Florence with the Giotto campanile, Venice and
its gondolas. She stopped, and her gaze immediately focused
on an Egyptian scarab made from terra cotta, placed in the
middle of the store window above a little mirror. The mirror
reflected the underbelly of the scarab, covered with fascinating
Egyptian hieroglyphics.

The desire to possess that object, which represented the
culmination of all of her desires, was so strong that it pushed
her to enter the shop and ask its price. Unfortunately she
didn't have much money with her, and who knew how much
that little *marvel* was worth. As she started to move away,
indecisive and disappointed, a young man came forward from
the dusky shadow of the shop and, with a smile and gesture,
invited here to enter: "Come in," he said to her in Arabic, but
the girl only understood the gesture.

She hesitated for a moment, but the suffocating heat of the
street and the fresh darkness of the interior compelled her to
cross the threshold. The young man immediately offered her a
stool, and she sat down, wanting to immediately ask the price
of the scarab she had seen in the window.

Would he be able to understand her? The young man,
dressed in white with a black *trabusc* on his head, had dark
olive skin and fleshy lips. He must certainly be an Arab. However, he looked at her and smiled, then asked: "Italian?" She
nodded yes and he asked again, in perfect Italian: "Are you
from the Circus?"

"From the Circus?" she thought, astonished. "But, no…I'm just passing by."

Maybe a caravan of jugglers had recently passed through the area. The dark-haired young woman was wearing large hoops in her ears and several necklaces, she did have a bit of a gypsy look to her. They sat in silence for a few moments, then the young man—who was only twenty five years old but appeared to be a mature adult to her, due to his black bushy whiskers—took a flower from a glass brimming with water. He offered her the fresh red carnation. Then, looking through the bundles of prints he had on the counter, he chose a few and handed them to her, saying: "Read these. You'll learn a few interesting things. But don't show them to anyone else."

The young woman glanced at the titles of the sheets of paper before her, and smiled: a few months ago, when she was working in a print shop, a workmate, who she remembered well, had led her to these same ideas of freedom. Such ideas, in her mind, had found fertile soil where they could sprout and grow. She thought: "Even in the Land of the Pharaohs, destiny once again brings me to cross paths with these rebels?"

She took the printed pages, folded them, placed them in her handbag and rose. *Should I ask the man how much the scarab costs now?* she thought. But she didn't have the courage.

He spontaneously held out his hand to the young woman.

"Thanks," she said, heading towards the door.

He held her small hand in his for a moment and asked, almost timidly: "Will you come back? Tomorrow?"

She nodded yes and soon found herself back in the blazing sun, after glancing back once more at the Egyptian scarab.

—

She didn't go back the next day, but instead collected all of the money she had so she could buy that *treasure*. After three days she went out, alone, but had a hard time finding the tiny little street where the nice salesman's shop was located. She had pinned the red carnation to her bosom, which was covered by a white cloth suit, as if it would make it easier for him to recognize and remember her. But she didn't really think that he had already forgotten about her.

The street wasn't deserted as it was the first time she had walked down it. Instead, a group of people stood observing, intrigued by something, right in front of that store. She came closer and saw immediately that everything inside of the shop had been broken, strewn about, destroyed, as if a cyclone had passed through. The sheets of paper with the stamps, the scenes of Italian cities, everything had been ripped to bits, as well as the few bookcases and counter. And right at the door stood two *Khedivial*-looking guards, holding rifles, keeping watch with an absent, impassible attitude.

The young woman shuddered, heartbroken: she came as close as she could to the window, sure that she would also see the scarab beetle broken into tiny pieces. But, ironically, or perhaps as a challenge to her, the scarab was still there among the ruins, tipped over, but still intact.

Before walking away, the young woman stopped amongst the little group of gawkers gathered there, near the unhinged door. She heard a few comments and words exchanged that filled her with despondency. They said that the police had destroyed a *cell* of subversives that had been hiding bombs, and almost all of them were Italian. Even the owner of this shop? Sure, all of their kind were like that. If they didn't sentence them to prison, they'd kick them all out of Egypt, no doubt.

The young woman, remembering the sincere eyes of the young stranger she had met three days earlier, felt a deep sorrow. What would become of him? And, with the unconscious egoism that many youth have, she thought: "Judging from the papers he gave me to read, I should have figured he was a *compagno*. I should have been brave enough to ask him about that scarab." And she walked away with her heart aching.[23]

***

---

23   Leda Rafanelli, *Liberazione*, unpublished manuscript, date unknown, 5–8. Fondo "LR-MM-MLF" conserved at the ABC.

In Italian usage, a *compagno* (plural: *compagni*) is different than a friend: it is someone with whom one shares an intellectual, ideological, or other type of affinity—somewhat like a comrade, but without the association to Marxism or socialism. One's schoolmates are *compagni di classe,* one's traveling partners are *compagni di viaggio.* One of Leda's anarchist *compagni* was Luigi Polli (1870–1922), the man with the scarab, who did live in Alexandria from 1896–1900, where he worked as a bookseller.[24] Leda would later reencounter Luigi in Florence, and they married in 1902. Given the anarchist ideal of free love, disdain for state-sponsored institutions—including marriage—and Luigi's full acceptance of Leda's other romantic relationships during twenty years of marriage (divorce was not legal at that time), not to mention the fact that they didn't live together for most of that time, if at all, it seems likely that their union was based more on friendship and protection, than romance.

It seems quite natural that Leda would fall in with the Italian community of anarchists in Alexandria. Yet what about her contact with Islam? Curiously, even in her autobiographical writings, Leda does not explain exactly how she came to discover and convert to the Muslim faith. She would go on to learn Arabic and even teach the language later in her life, yet chances are she did not already speak Egyptian Arabic in 1900: her impressions of local religious life during her time in Egypt were likely based on non-literary sources.

It was not unheard of for European expatriates or even anarchists to travel to North Africa and "convert" to the local culture or religion. The Swedish painter Ivan Aguéli (1869–1917), for example, was active in anarchist circles in France, where he converted to Islam in 1898 before traveling to Egypt and joining the Shadhiliyah Arabiyah Sufi order.[25] Henri Gustave Jossot (1866–1951) was another leftist who converted to Islam after moving to Tunisia in 1911, referring to his new religion as having "no mystery, no dogma, no clergy, almost no rituals, the most rational of all religions; thus I adopted it, judging that a creature does not need to go through the intermediation of any priests in order to adore his Creator."[26]

---

24   M. Antonioli. et al, (directors), *Dizionario Biografico degli Anarchici Italiani,* Volume 1 (Pisa: BFS Edizioni, 2003), 368–9.
25   Biography, the Ivan Anguéli website, http://www.ivanagueli.com/biography.html.
26   Henri-Gustave Jossot, "*Sauvages Blancs,*" http://gustave.jossot.free.fr/sauvages_blancs.html.

No matter what the influence, Leda adopted Islam on her own terms. Her library contained plenty of Arabic language books, including a copy of the Qur'an, and as she mentions throughout her personal recollections, she gradually taught herself to read and write Arabic. Given her penchant for individualism and autodidactism, it's not hard to imagine how she could have drawn her own conclusions and made up her own interpretations of Islam; given her anarchist principles, she certainly would not have wanted any official institution or authoritative voice to govern her spiritual practice.

Considering how much fantasy Leda seems to have incorporated in creating her Muslim world—over the years, her portraits consistently show not just the kohl and earrings, but also her wardrobe full of long, flowing robes and headscarves as she poses against a background (her house) full of embroidered tapestries, low tables and rugs, and various religious paraphernalia—it's obvious that she was not pursuing a conservative or fundamentalist interpretation. Some scholars call Leda a Sufi, though she never identified as one nor did she seem interested in seeking the legitimacy or label of any particular sect (Sufi or Shiite or Sunni or otherwise) in order to further define her Islam.

Leda's conversion to and practice of Islam took place entirely outside of the mosque or a concrete religious community. She essentially undertook a nondenominational and institution-free practice of religion, though she did study the Qur'an well enough to cite it in her writings. Despite her visual "exhibitionism," as evidenced through the photographic legacy she enthusiastically created throughout her life, she remained relatively demure on the issue: while she adjusted her dress and diet to what she considered to be Islamic standards, she never proselytized or embarked upon conversion campaigns: indeed, it would have been difficult to convert her fellow anarchists to any kind of religion.

Her Muslim identity was at best tolerated by her largely atheist comrades, but, conversely, she had absolutely no qualms with their lack of faith or atheist lifestyles. A lot of what we do know of her beliefs and practice of Islam comes from the many children's books and fables she wrote, set in Islamic countries or cultures, during the last forty years of her life. Her work gives us glimpses of how her interpretation of Islam changed with time, as she did, but the inherently mystical element of her faith seems to have remained a lifelong truth: "Since I was a child, I have always said, with firm conviction, that I was 'born a millenarian.' All of my intimate 'memories,' dreams, aspirations, desires were based, defined, oriented towards Ancient Egypt, my adopted Homeland."[27]

It could be argued that Leda's interpretation of Islam was also shaped as a rebellion against the European world—industrialized, obsessed with money, power, status, hierarchy—through her alliance with an Eastern world (just as much a stereotyped fiction, however, as the idea of a single Western world), seemingly shrouded in an indifference to the modern world and deeply rooted in ancient wisdom.

In Chapter 5, we will explore more of Leda's writings on Islam, as well as the philosophical links between anarchism and Islam. What is important to remember here is that Leda's conversion to both Islam and anarchism, which appear to have both taken place as she transitioned into adulthood, gave her a distinct cultural identity and commitment. In her public life, she joined the fight against institutions. In her private life, she worked to develop a religious vision that made sense to her and fulfilled her spiritual needs. It's commonly perceived that anarchism and religion are like oil and water; yet Leda, who often called herself *contro-corrente*, or someone who swims against the tide, was never one to live within predefined rules. Indeed, the basic principles of anarchism are fairly simple and not necessarily opposed to religion: a belief in the abolition of authority, government and/or hierarchy; a belief in the power of the individual; and a belief in some form or another of collective cooperation, whether it be large-scale coordination controlled from the bottom upward, small-scale participative democracy, or simply non-hierarchical collectivism.

Leda's ideas on anarchism were not oriented towards the practical construction of a utopian society nor towards the conversion of new recruits for the civilization of the future, but instead focused on supporting the natural development of humans, free from the oppression of social constructs:

> It was our dream, perhaps even our noble Utopia, and it's
> still our unattainable goal: to create, all around the world,
> a stronger and more aware Humanity, different from the
> oppressed, cowardly and aching throng of people who haven't
> understood how much beauty, how much truth, how much

27   Leda Rafanelli, *Memorie di una Chiromante*, edt. M.M. Cappellini (Cuneo: Nerosubianco, 2010), 5.

good there is in Life. For many centuries, this reality has been understood by liberated and superior Humans, who have done all they could to teach us about it with their words, their examples and even by sacrificing their lives. Throughout the ages, individuals have tried to break down the criminal ignorance of the masses resigned to slavery—previously chained to the galley's oars, then bent under the heavy yoke of exploited labor, and always, even today, thwarted by every kind of law, which always works in favor of their masters. Despite all of the hubbub over "social welfare," the class struggle continues.

We have always strived to enlighten morally backwards people with ideas of freedom: and by "backwards" we don't mean people living in other countries whose traditions diverge from European customs yet who, nevertheless, have their own proper Civilizations and have been defending them for centuries against the military invasions of predatory Nations. Rather the backwards masses are amongst us, opposed to thoughts and hopes for individual freedom. They must convince themselves that for some people resistance is futile, that seeking understanding and consensus in order to enjoy a better life is useless. We can only come together with Men who believe in ideas of freedom, who scorn all of the falseness produced by easing into the illusion of an effortless, comfortable, "modern" life. As members of a new Humanity, we absolutely detest all that is not sincere.

We know that this insurmountable distance between us and conformist, religious, militaristic society runs deep. Its version of reality is not only engraved in the textbooks used in State schools, but has been preached since time immemorial. As internationalists, we do not limit ourselves to national affairs: our heroes, our martyrs, our warriors are from all ages. From avengers to thinkers, poets to dynamic propagandists: every individual gave all they had to the Cause of Anarchism, the best of their minds and souls. A true Anarchist does not get caught up in petty arguments with fellow *compagni*, she understands that rebels must be united by their Ideas as in a free community built upon thought and struggle. There is only one objective: to fight against everything that creates poverty and evil, the giant lie of the society we live in. And our enemies are well-organized, they support each other, protecting and defending themselves to hide their crimes and their lies. Yet we—a new Humanity—continue to struggle and keep our resistance alive with all of our means, actions and thoughts. From Harmodius to Bresci, to Armand, to the most obscure *compagno*.

[...] We feel so different, so far removed, as enemies of this vile humanity that accepts everything and allows itself to be ordered about, controlled, taken advantage of—all in the name of the Law!

And, unfortunately, these Laws were designed by crafty, selfish people. Laws that regulate all human activity, related to every aspect of social life! Yet only the laws of Nature should be accepted, considered, studied by individuals who are aware and intelligent; since only these Laws are eternal and ineluctable. And we know this from the experience of all people from all times.[28]

---

28   Leda Rafanelli, *L'Umanità Nuova* (unpublished manuscript, date unknown), 1–3. Fondo "LR-MM-MLF" conserved at the ABC.

CHAPTER III
The Vocation of Propaganda

Finally, after long hours of brisk marching, quickening his pace again and again to ward off the danger of frostbite, the darkness dissolved in the East as the livid sky announced the new day.

The winter dawn is so dismal that a longing for golden summer days vibrates through people and things. He turned around and looked over his shoulder at the city behind him, as if he was unsure whether to retrace his steps or to keep going forward.

He shrugged his shoulders and continued onward.

He didn't like big cities. Wild and rebellious, he felt uneasy on the crowded, noisy streets, and would hurry toward the suburbs, to the working-class neighborhoods, where his shabby clothes and worn shoes went unnoticed among the other workers. But the presence of the big city still loomed over the suburbs.

The streets were wide, life was illuminated, and the sensation of movement was overwhelming.

Factories sprung up like weeds, machine shops swallowed three or four hundred workers every morning. Industrial plants, workshops and buildings were being built everywhere you looked. Lorenzo had passed through crowds of laborers and drifters looking for work, because not everyone, even in the rich city, had a job year-round.

His attempts to find something were all in vain. While eating a meager meal in a greasy spoon, he had asked his table

mate, a thin and pale young man with shifty eyes, where he
could find a cheap hotel. He wanted to spend one last day
looking for work, now with the desire to make money rather
than to perfect his craft as a mechanical blacksmith, though
if he could master a craft, he would be free and more sure of
himself in the future.

But when he woke up the next morning, he realized he
had been robbed of the few pennies left in his pocket and
shoes. His bag of books had been left alone. By sheer luck,
before going to sleep he had taken off his jacket, which held
his wallet, papers, and five lira, and folded it in half to use as
a pillow.

That's how he had managed to save what he had left.

He asked the hotelkeeper for an explanation, but the man
barely listened to him. He didn't even think to report the miserable theft: instead he paid, breaking his last five lira note,
and left the hotel barefoot, his socks in his pocket. After a few
hours of looking around, he bought a pair of used shoes full
of nails from someone selling them on the street. He walked
along and passed a bathhouse, and decided to allow himself
the luxury of a hot bath. As evening approached, he had only
visited a few machine shops in his search for work. But there
were more than enough hands to go around. He found himself without a place to sleep and, disappointed, he decided to
start back down the road.

After resting in an abandoned market stall, he resumed
walking through the snow, across the countryside. He was
now even hungrier, more exhausted, but his face exuded a
tranquility as serene as his soul.

—

[...] A little while later he heard the sound of wheels, and in
the distance, further down the straight road, he saw a milk
wagon coming toward him. It carried a colossal flask of milk
encircled with copper and equipped with a faucet, seemingly squeezed into the barouche, slowly swaying although the
horse was moving rather quickly.

Just as the vehicle was passing him, Lorenzo felt the insidious cramps of hunger convulse in his stomach. Almost mechanically, compelled by his desire for a drop of milk, he gestured for the cart's driver to stop.

He was astonished to see that it was a child, perhaps just ten years old, driving the wagon. The boy was wrapped up in a heavy cloak and his baby face already had the sly, shrewd guise of a merchant.

Lorenzo had noticed that in this region, women and children, even little girls, all worked busily, stricken with the fever for profit. He had seen nine-year-old laborers carrying heaps of bricks on their tiny shoulders as they climbed up the unsteady staircases of houses under construction, and small errand boys racing through the city on bicycles loaded up with bundles to deliver. He had seen little girls in short petticoats standing at the counters in the shops, completely serious, understanding the importance of their position, and making change for their customers after double checking what they had received and counting what they gave back. But that horse, that vat of milk entrusted to a child at that hour in the morning, when the boy should have been in bed in the arms of his mother, made him think sorrowfully about the uselessness of childhood in cities full of traffic and work.

He didn't realize that some children are better at doing business than adults!

Meanwhile, the young milkman looked at Lorenzo, waiting for him to tell him what he wanted. He had clear, cold blue eyes that appeared to be empty.

"Give me a penny's worth of milk," the man finally said, shaken from his thoughts by another stomach cramp.

"I'm not selling it," responded the child in dialect. "I'm taking it to the dairy shops."

"So what? No one would notice if you were down a glass of milk. Do you have a measuring cup?"

"Yes," responded the child, showing him a one-liter container.

"Give me some inside of that. I'm hungry."

He thought that his manner of speaking would move the child to pity him. But instead, upon hearing those words, the child looked at him suspiciously. He had been about to step down, but now he withdrew the leg he had planted on the footboard.

"And the penny?" he asked.

"Here!" Lorenzo answered, showing him his last coin, his heart aching.

The little milkman got down and placed the measuring cup underneath the faucet. He poured out a bit of milk, looked at it, and as it appeared to not be enough, even to him, he gingerly released a few more drops. He held out his hand as he passed the measuring cup to Lorenzo.

"The penny," he repeated.

Lorenzo felt the urge to punch him. What a self-centered little brat!

He took the milk and drank it, while the child looked at him with the eyes of a gendarme.

Then it occurred to Lorenzo that he might save that penny for a piece of bread and punish this greedy, money-hungry boy at the same time. He could clearly tell that this was not a poor stable boy the master would mistreat if he did not bring home enough money in the evening. No, he was a child who was already making money, who went off and had fun on Sundays, who was maybe even the son of the man who owned the dairy. And Lorenzo decided to leave after draining the cup.

"The penny?"

The child's voice was so cold and haughty that the man almost felt ashamed. He took the penny back out of his pocket and gave it to the boy. The boy looked at the coin, pulled out a leather purse, placed it inside (he also had a watch with a chain) and without giving the traveler another glance got back on the box seat, wrapped himself up in the cloak, whipped his horse and went away. And Lorenzo stood, motionless, watching the boy leave with his last penny, his piece of bread for the day that had just begun. And he felt such bitter disdain for that lack of generosity in a young boy, seemingly so focused on his own interests, that he was suddenly filled with the desire to hurl stones after him.[1]

---

1   Leda Rafanelli, *L'Eroe della Folla,* (Milan: Casa Editrice Sociale, 1920), 18–23.

***

The Hero of the Masses (*L'Eroe della folla*) was published in 1920, telling the story of Lorenzo, an orphan raised by a peasant family in central Italy, who sets out to seek his fortune in the industrialized landscape, encountering greed, injustice, dishonesty, and lots of bad luck along the way. The narrative shows that his unpleasant experiences are direct consequences of a hierarchical state and exploitative capitalism. His story, that of a young man facing the tumult and hardships of the modern world, is woven around useful illustrations and practical definitions of sabotage, insurrection, solidarity, strikes, and other tools of resistance. The novel exemplifies a literary style—political, instructive, character-focused narrative—that Leda developed as a natural offshoot of a more blatant, inflammatory style used for writing propaganda, a craft she earnestly dedicated herself to after joining the anarchist movement in Florence in the early years of the twentieth century.

The word "propaganda" had rather tame connotations in the early twentieth century, a far cry from the manipulative brainwashing it is synonymous with today. Mark Crispin Miller traces the genesis of the word back to 1622, when Pope Gregory XV launched a new initiative to combat Protestantism through propagating the Catholic faith.[2] At that time, propaganda was simply a way to spread the good news, and was not synonymous with "subversive falsehood," as it has been since the 1910s, when misleading information was aggressively broadcasted, in several different countries, in order to manipulate the general public into thinking that intervention in the global conflict of WWI was not only necessary, but desirable. Leda's use of the word "propaganda" has nothing to do with lies or deception: much as Pope Gregory XV intended to use his propaganda to describe and explain the principles of his faith, anarchists used their propaganda to describe and illustrate the ideas and perspectives of their movement.

Leda's propaganda could be understood as a form of pulp fiction: cheaply produced and widely accessible (due to its low or even free price) reading entertainment for the masses, focused on themes that reflected anarchist causes and convictions. The nonfiction propaganda she produced, in the form of critical essays or calls to action, was more directly focused on encouraging the reader to specifically do (or stop doing)

---

2   Mark Miller, Crispin in Bernays, Edward. *Propaganda* (Brooklyn: Ig publishing, 2005), 11.

something, yet in no cases was her work intended to infringe upon an individual's freedom of choice and association, which would be inherently contradictory to the anarchist cause. Malatesta succinctly describes the craft of propaganda as practiced by anarchists:

> Our task is to push people to demand and seize all of the freedom they can grasp, to make themselves responsible for providing for their own needs without waiting for orders from any kind of authority. Our task is to demonstrate the uselessness and harmfulness of government, to provoke and to encourage, through speech and through action, all good individual and collective initiatives.
>
> It is, therefore, a question of education in freedom, of making people who are accustomed to obedience and passivity consciously aware of their own strength and abilities. We have to encourage people to do things for themselves, or at least think they are acting on their own initiative and inspiration even when their actions are actually suggested by others, just like how a good school teacher, when he presents a problem his pupil cannot solve immediately, helps the pupil so that he thinks he has found the solution on his own, thus acquiring courage and confidence in his own abilities. This is what we should do with our propaganda.[3]

Around 1900, Leda shifted her base of literary and political activity to Florence, at the time a major nucleus for Italian anarchism and syndicalism.[4] In the first decades of the twentieth century, radical circles found a home in the *camera del lavoro*, or labor bureau, which was not a government department, but something that could better be described as a union hall, not exclusive to one specific union, modeled after the French *bourses du travail*. There were *camere da lavoro* in most Italian cities from 1895 through the 1920s, and the spaces served as headquarters

---

3   Errico Malatesta, *Scritti: Volume III* (Geneva: Edizione del "Risveglio," 1936) 400–401.

4   It might seem logical that she lived with Polli in the city or its environs, but no records exist regarding her residential status until she moved to Milan in 1909. It's also entirely possible she still lived, at least part of the time, with her family in Pistoia, which is located 40 km away from Florence.

for political and labor groups. Ideas were shared and new collaborations formed in these horizontal social institutions.

The Florentine *camera da lavoro* was informally presided over by Giuseppe Scarlatti (1854–1916), who had worked with Turati to found the Italian socialist party and movement. Within this milieu, Leda had the opportunity to rub elbows with the veterans of the First International while attending meetings and rallies. She took on one of her first major roles as an organizer by coordinating meetings, conferences, publications and membership for an assistance committee for political victims (*comitato pro vittime politiche*), which provided support to people suffering from the state's political repression. Leda further built up her profile as a social activist by cofounding the Porta a Prato anticlerical circle, which brought together syndicalists and anarchists. She began keeping correspondence with subversives all over the country, although she would never meet some of these compagni in person.

In its earliest incarnations, Leda's propaganda seems to be inspired by *verismo*, a popular style of literary realism used by Italian writers such as Giovanni Verga and Salvatore DiGiacomo during the late nineteenth century to objectively photograph social reality. Her work was based upon what she had seen and experienced, as well as the people she encountered through her public activities: attending one meeting after another, participating in demonstrations, selling her pamphlets on the street, and working in the print shops and eventually publishing houses she co-founded with friends. *Verismo*, however, required the author's objectivity and abstention from social critique; Leda did not take on this mantle of impartiality.[5] Rather, she used her sketches of reality as a vehicle for promoting anarchist ideology.

Aside from being easily digestible from an intellectual point of view, the small format of these sketches also allowed the material to be used or reused as a pamphlet. Leda printed both straightforward calls to action as well as her fiction in her pamphlets, and at a time when the average working-class person could not afford to go around collecting books, this provided a more effective way for her stories to reach her readers.

Scanning the titles of pamphlets Leda published in the first decade of the twentieth century provides an overview of the various messages she sought to transmit through her work:

---

5   *La storia della letteratura italiana scritta da Antonio Piromalli,* http://www. storiadellaletteratura.it/main.php?cap=18&par=4.

The confession
The prince's bastard daughter: A crowned mother and a
plebeian mother
The hymn of humanity. Thinking of Luigia Pezzi
Loving and fighting. A social folktale
Freedom for the victims of reactionary activity and hunger
To Italian mothers
Against schools
From "God" to freedom
The crown and la blouse (a social conflict)
Strong arms: Propaganda pamphlet against the construction
of new prisons
The last martyr of free thought: Francisco Ferrer
The bourgeois school
A tragedy
Against dogma
Clerical chastity
Modern anti-clericalism
Who is the tsar?
The barracks...school of the nation. From a soldier's diary
Workers! To laborers in the machine shop. To those who work
on ships, in the fields, underground. To those who resist,
to the pariahs. To humble people of low birth. To the
corrupted[6]

Some of the pamphlets listed above were short essays focused on presenting the logic behind a certain anarchist principle or value, and others
were short, anonymous snapshots featuring everyday characters fighting against oppression from authoritative institutions. The latter were
eventually published in two collections: *For Our Ideas* (*Per l'idea nostra*),
published in 1905, and *Social Sketches*, published in 1910. As opposed
to the single plot of *The Hero of the Masses*, *Social Sketches* was comprised
of about sixty stand-alone chapters each five to six pages long and with
a clear, succinct message regarding one specific social or political issue.
Each chapter took place in a different setting—the factory, the field, the
church, the schoolroom, the insane asylum, the mine, the brothel, the

6   Alessandra Pierotti, *Leda Rafanelli. Tra letteratura e anarchia. Atti del convengo*,
     edt. Fiamma Chessa (Reggio Emilia: Biblioteca Panizzi, 2008), 187–188.

convent—covering as much ground as possible and outlining the numerous applications of anarchist principles in everyday scenarios, as well as the many faces of oppression induced by the authorities in charge, whether economic, political, ecclesiastical, intellectual, or all in the family. Rarely do any of the characters have names, nor are the cities or years pinpointed; narrated in third person, these sketches are rendered as templates that the reader can hopefully apply to his or her life in order to finally understand the mechanisms at work behind the misery or oppression experienced in an everyday context.

Aside from spreading her message through pamphlets, Leda, like many of her fellow anarchists, flooded the independent press with contributions of articles and stories, eventually going on to edit and produce a few of her own newspapers and journals. On a par with pamphlets in terms of usefulness for diffusing propaganda, although slightly more expensive and somewhat dependent upon subscriptions and pro-bono printing, hundreds of these periodicals popped up in the early twentieth century, some lasting for just a few issues and others lasting for years. Writers for these newspapers and journals were generally unpaid: the return was in making a contribution to public debate, expressing one's personal point of view, and practicing the art of eloquent argumentation. Very few newspapers were diffused nationally in Italy prior to WWI, and therefore the location where a newspaper was based, not to mention the ideology of its editorial staff, often had significant effects on raising awareness and understanding of current events and issues within the local area.

The personality of each periodical reflected the general persuasion of the editors behind it and thus the ideology promoted by the publication was explicitly declared on the front page. Although government sequestrations were frequent, anyone who had something to say, no matter how subversive, could find at least one paper or journal willing to print their perspective.

One of Leda's first major collaborations (meaning, regular and prolific) was with the monthly journal *La Blouse* (April 1906–April 1910), whose slogan was "The emancipation of workers must be engineered by the workers themselves." The journal was presented as if was written by manual laborers—with just a little help from the anarchist editors—for a readership from the same demographic, creating a mouthpiece for revolutionary, syndicalist, and nonconformist voices straight from the blue-collar ranks. However, the high level of intellectualism and the topics of debates presented in the articles didn't quite match up with the average level of education most working-class writers would probably have had, or could likely have achieved on their own through self-study in the quarry, thus it is generally believed that these contributions were written by Leda and her literary compagni who, although they may have worked the typesetting machines, represented a different kind of manual laborer entirely. Featuring first-person descriptions of working conditions, reports on recent demonstrations and strikes, obituaries of syndicalist leaders, discussions of educational initiatives, political poems, book reviews, acknowledgments to recent donors and theoretical essays, *La Blouse* provided a common forum for exploring the everyday realities of workers while advocating for syndicalism and, eventually, revolution.

Other papers followed a different model, such as *Vir* (1907–1908), edited by Leda and a young anarchist named Giuseppe Monanni (1887—1952) right at the start of their domestic partnership. Monanni, described as a shy, introverted person whose conversational contributions were often monosyllabic, nevertheless spent most of his life writing and publishing tirelessly against the tyranny of militarism, clericalism, and economic injustice. Barely twenty years old when he left his native Arezzo for Florence, he was already a committed antimilitarist and individualist anarchist. Like Leda, he was an autodidact and typographer by trade, and had also worked for a political victims assistance committee, defending political activists imprisoned after insurrections in 1894 and 1899 and in particular after Bresci's regicide in 1900. Leda had separated from Luigi Polli by the time Monanni came along, and given their shared political interests, similar backgrounds as independent scholars, and mutual passion and skill for editorial and publishing initiatives, Leda and Monanni felt an immediate affinity and fell in love in no time.

Vir, a new magazine of lofty social questions, literature, art, and science came out monthly (more or less) and represented an entirely new take on anarchism, moving away from the usual propaganda and discussions of current strikes and demonstrations.[7] Featuring articles with titles such as *Theory of knowledge and individualism* and *Anarchism, Hellenic sources and the Sophists*, it reflected a more intellectual conception of anarchism, focusing on ideas and art rather than mass action, promoting the individualist anarchism that Leda and Monanni were among the first to

---

7   Leonardo Bettini, *Bibliografia dell'anarchismo* Volume I, tome 1 (Florence: CP editrice 1972).

outwardly advocate in Italy, although each by their own interpretation. Indeed, in Monanni's own words, the individualism behind *Vir* reflected a deeper deconstruction of revolutionary values: "We are against society as it has been constructed, and against all associative constructions [...], anarchy and socialism basically strive to establish, by either generalizing their principles through decree or through education, the same principle of justice that inform our current society."[8] Hence, *Vir* set out to explore what values would be important under conditions of freedom, rather than in light of current social struggles.

By 1907 Leda had made a name for herself not only with her writing but also for her unique expression of anarchist identity, and she was invited to write the foreword to *Our individualism and other individualisms* (*Il nostro e l'altrui individualismo*), a book written by Armando Borghi (1882–1968) to defend the nascent individualist strain of anarchism from its critics, who considered it to be too conducive to amoralism and entirely counterproductive (see Chapter 6 for a more in-depth discussion of individualist anarchism). Leda's publishing collaborations expanded in all directions. Benefitting from the technical and literary training she had received during her years working in print shops, Leda had opened her first publishing house with Polli in 1904, the Casa Editrice Rafanelli-Polli.

The Casa Editrice Rafanelli-Polli printed anarchist pamphlets as well as books (many written by Leda herself) against the church, army, schools, and prisons, and served as a point of cultural reference for local anarchists. It operated out of a big room on Via Panzani, where Leda wrote and did the page setting, with a small retail outlet on Via Borgo Ognissanti, where Luigi oversaw sales. From the little information available and few surviving pamphlets, it appeared as if the majority of the output from the Casa Editrice Rafanelli-Polli was anarchist propaganda, unlike the more philosophical, historical, and literary works Leda would release through the publishing houses she would co-direct in Milan a few years later.

***

It was already well into the morning and Lorenzo, refreshed by those few drops of milk, continued walking. With the onset

---

8   Antonioli, M; Berti, G; Fedele, S; Iuso, P (directors), *Dizionario Biografico degli Anarchici Italiani* Volume 2 (Pisa: BFS Edizioni, 2004), 7.

of the harsh season, the workers had deserted the fields, and
when he finally saw a cluster of houses he headed toward them,
thinking he needed to find some bread, whatever the cost.

The muddy gray road stretched out, straight and narrow,
seemingly into infinity. Each step heavier than the last, Lorenzo continued onwards, his head down and his gaze focused on
the ground. His eye was caught by the red splotch of a shredded, crumpled piece of paper sticking out from the muck, its
bold black letters showing through between the creases.

He bent down to pick the paper up and unfolded it out
of curiosity. It was half of a *strike* pamphlet. He couldn't tell
where it came from. But it must have been written by revolu-
tionaries, as it ended with these words:

"Strikers! If the ruling class responds to your united action
with police and prison, if bourgeois arrogance forces you to
return to work out of hunger, remember that your hands still
hold a weapon you can use against the bourgeoisie: *sabotage!*"

After he finished reading, Lorenzo carefully folded the
shredded pamphlet back up and slipped it into his bun-
dle. The words pleased him, and repeating them to himself
brought him a sense of satisfaction.

As an apprentice, following the example provided by his
master, he had taken up the habit of reading. Thus he was
no longer an ignorant peasant who understood nothing and
thought about nothing. His adolescence coincided with the
awakening of the proletariat consciousness amidst the first
battles between capital and labor. Together with his master and the other apprentices, he had observed the popular
uprisings and studied the works that discussed revolts and
evolution toward a better future. Lorenzo immediately knew
what that little shred of the subversive pamphlet meant when
it suggested workers resort to *sabotage*.

Sabotage was the double-edged sword first devised by the
French railroad worker Sabot, then embraced by the more
antagonistic factions of workers' organizations in France
when, reduced to extreme measures during their resistance,
striking workers were forced to return to work. The very instruments of labor were the target of *sabotage*: the machines,

the production processes—*sabotage* meant damage, destruction, ruining everything in the name of revenge and retaliatory action, blatant action that required its perpetrator to maintain secrecy. The worker-*saboteur* blended in with the crowd: an individual who worked for the good of a community of peers. And the blame was not borne by the saboteur himself, but by everyone.

A smile brightened the traveller's face. The word *sabotage* made him think of something that had happened when he was an adolescent.

He remembered an unconscious act of sabotage he had performed when he was a young lad—an act that proved to be disastrous for several landowners in his village while the field and farm workers were conducting a general strike. And that memory always made him smile.

He saw himself again as a farm boy, twelve or thirteen years old, enthusiastic like all young people, excited to witness the farmers' rebellion, the first he had ever experienced. The revolutionary period had begun with violent uprisings in Sicily and ended with the bloody May of 1898. In the countryside where Lorenzo lived, the *fascio operaio* had suddenly called a farm workers' strike during the early days of spring, and it was now at risk of ending in a crushing defeat.[9] The landowners had been able to carry on with work as usual using a few strikebreakers recruited from outside of the region, as the season when the workers were needed the most—the harvest—was still some time away, thus the owners didn't feel any pressure to yield to the workers' demands. During the season of germination, the land works for humans. After a harsh and dry winter, the bountiful rains of March had nourished the grain, now budding, thick and promising. And the striking workers realized they had picked a bad time to take action.

Then the propagandists, sent to the region by the socialist party, advised them to save the strike by making it a *solidarity* strike and extending it to other types of workers, an idea that

---

9   A *fascio operaio* was a type of labor league that sprung up in various parts of Italy during the 1870s.

was enthusiastically received. And so the dairy workers joined the struggle, alongside the cattle herders and many tenant farmers who worked the land for the demanding owners. The haymakers had gone on strike first, making it difficult to keep the troughs full, and within a week the barns were empty. The next day, the innocent and anxious animals tied to the empty troughs started to moan. The few *volunteers*, small-time land owners who thought it would be easy to replace the strikers by milking the heifers and looking after the cattle, found themselves bewildered with just a few armfuls of grass and straw to divide amongst hundreds of famished animals, whose moaning almost sounded like human wailing.

Some of the *owners* themselves, helped by domestic servants, stooped to tend to their horses. But their efforts were in vain.

Cattle breeding was a major activity in that region and paid very well, thus the strike of the cattle workers and stable hands who worked at the manor farms could not continue for one more day without causing serious damage. At four o'clock in the afternoon, the landowners had a long meeting with representatives of the striking workers, yet the negotiations went nowhere. The owners refused to discuss the issues or accommodate any of the exploited workers' meek demands. And the animals—locked up inside the deserted stables— drove the landowners and their volunteers away with bellows of starving fury. The situation only grew worse.

As the evening drew near, the town buzzed with the news that the chief of police in the city had received a telegraph requesting reinforcements. Then came the rumors: the soldiers had already arrived and were secretly hiding in the mansions of the biggest landowners, who were frightened by the threatening and violent words speakers were using at the rallies. Everyone was sure that the soldiers had not been called in merely to *restore order*, but also to mow the grass, gather the hay hidden in the barns of the striking croppers, fill the troughs with water, and milk the cows and goats. The soldiers would work as farmhands for the comfort and peace of their lords.

But nobody had seen the soldiers yet.

In the evening, the strikers assembled as usual in the piazza, and the speaker spoke from the window of the house of Matteo, the blacksmith, who had offered his home to the commission and the socialists. A few carabinieri from the local garrison, powerless and unable to push through, ambled around the village with their rifles on their shoulders. The night was calm and serene, its normal silence interrupted by the unsettling, sorrowful and strange bellows of the starving animals.

Lying in his bed in a room on the ground floor, Lorenzo could not sleep that night. His window looked out over the moonlit fields, and the boy could clearly hear the moans of the poor beasts overcome with hunger. The soldiers would arrive in the morning, true, but so many would have suffered during the night: the fat heifers, the strong oxen, the horses and the donkeys chained to the empty troughs!

The boy felt pity for the innocent beasts that were being punished because humans couldn't come to an agreement. Earlier that morning, at the forge where he had now been working for several months, he had overheard the blacksmith and a propagandist talking about how the strike had been lost. The soldiers, intervening to save the animals, would weaken the strength of the cowhands, and the farmers would have to surrender.

Only a few hours remained before dawn. Lorenzo thought the soldiers would arrive with the sunrise, and then the animals would finally have their food. But why make them suffer any longer? The moans of the animals troubled Lorenzo so deeply he couldn't sleep. A sullen, especially long wail came from a nearby stable and disturbed him to the point that he decided to help that animal, just as he would help a poor person by an act of charity. The wail had come from Morella, a beautiful cow, still nursing her little calf just a few weeks old. And that anguished cry was truly a cry for help.

Lorenzo quietly got out of bed, but Nino, one of the boys who slept in the same room, woke up. He saw Lorenzo head towards the window and open it cautiously.

"Where are you going?" he asked.

"Be quiet, don't wake pops. Can't you hear how *Morella* is moaning? She's dying of hunger and still has a little one to look after."

Nino, too, was moved as he thought about how that frail little white calf, with its large head and sweet, dewy eyes, was being forced to die of hunger. He jumped out of bed and rushed to pull on his shirt and short pants. He went over to the window as Lorenzo was climbing out.

"Wait for me. I'm coming too."

A great peace had descended over the barnyard and the fields. The forest loomed in the distance, a black shadow against the creamy lunar sky. A few fireflies flashed their cold little flames through the budding wheat.

"There's no hay here," said Nino. "And the barns are empty."

But Lorenzo was heading towards a field of wheat. With rapid movements he grabbed large handfuls of the precious blades and piled them into Nino's arms.

"But this is wheat!"

"Mister Andrea won't be ruined by this," Lorenzo responded, softly. "And anyway, it's the owners' fault that the animals are suffering. Really, the strikers should burn all of this as revenge!"

"It would be hard to burn this wheat, it's full of dew."

"Then it's better to give it to these animals! There's always someone who needs it..."

They filled their arms with wheat and headed toward a nearby stall.[10]

***

Among the many colorful characters of the Florentine scene, Leda's friends, compagni, and editorial collaborators represented a wide range of people, many of whom she considered her adopted family. She was particularly close to Maria Luisa Minguzzi (1852–1911), "a splendidly beautiful woman, tall, robust, shapely, with a frank and open temperament, quick and straightforward with her words, who charmed all who

10   Leda Rafanelli, *L'Eroe della Folla*, 32–38.

came near her."[11] Minguzzi was one of the first to advocate socialist feminism in Italy, and her name became known after she printed a manifesto in 1876 calling upon women to fight against the discrimination and ignorance that destroyed their dignity. Her four decades of political activity were marred by several long stints in prison and work camps: when Leda met her during the first decade of the twentieth century, she was suffering from health problems and going blind after having spent a rough year in the Orbetello penal colony. Maria Luisa and her husband, Francesco Pezzi (1849–1917), worked on a variety of socialist, internationalist, and anarchist solidarity campaigns, and their home in Florence was nicknamed the "Vatican" of the anarchist elite.

Letters exchanged between Leda and another one of her compagni, Carlo Molaschi (1886–1953), were later published in a book, alongside letters he wrote to the woman he would eventually marry, Maria Rossi.[12] The closeness and sincerity of the friendship between Leda and Molaschi led to an extraordinary epistolary exchange, fed by their common background as writers/editors and proponents of individualist anarchism. Arrested for the first time at the age of fifteen for distributing subversive flyers in front of a theater during a general strike, Molaschi worked for years as an accountant while moonlighting as an anarchist activist. Notable among his many collaborations are his work with Luigi Molinari to design and create the Milanese "Modern School," based on the anarchist, working-class model developed by Spanish anarchist Francisco Ferrer (although the space and the funding had been secured, the project was quashed by the city government upon the outbreak of World War I).

Rafanelli was also very close, ideologically and personally, to Pietro Gori (1865–1911), a lawyer, activist, journalist, and prolific writer of fiction, nonfiction, speeches, poetry, songs, and plays. He was called the "vagabond knight" of anarchism due to his worldwide popularity, a result of multiple lecture tours across Europe, the United States, and the Middle East, not to mention his intensive work in fueling the worker's movement in Argentina.[13] Graduating with a law degree in 1889, Gori dedicated the rest of his life to the anarchist cause, yet still managed to

11   Antonioli, M; Berti, G; Fedele, S; Iuso, P (directors), *Dizionario Biografico degli Anarchici Italiani* Volume 2, 188.
12   Granata, M., *Lettere d'amore e d'amicizia. La corrispondenza di Leda Rafanelli, Carlo Molaschi e Maria Rossi (1913–1919)* (Pisa: BFS, 2002).
13   M. Antonioli, et al., *Dizionario Biografico degli Anarchici Italiani,* Volume 1, 750.

put his law degree to use as he often served as the defense attorney for his anarchist *compagni*, who frequently faced charges in court. The closing statements Gori wrote and delivered during these proceedings were so eloquent and well-developed that they were often subsequently published as anarchist propaganda. In the courtroom, he was known for introducing legal counter-attacks, flipping the roles and accusing liberticidal and bourgeois society of violence against the people.[14]

In addition to being an elegant orator, Gori's creative and eclectic style won audiences over everywhere he went. After finishing a lecture, he would usually take out his guitar and sing anarchist songs he had written himself.[15] The lyrics of *Farewell Lugano* (*Addio a Lugano*), written in 1895, are typical of the brief yet clear messages he expressed through his music, rendered here without the charm of their rhyme in Italian:

> Farewell beautiful Lugano
> oh sweet, giving land,
> now the anarchists are leaving,
> shooed away for no reason.
> And as they leave they sing
> with hope in their hearts.
> And as they leave they sing
> with hope in their hearts.
> And it's for you, the oppressed,
> for you, the workers,
> For you that we've been handcuffed
> by the evil wretches.
> And yet our idea
> is just an idea of love.
> And yet our idea
> is just an idea of love.

Despite all of this creativity and constructive activism, outside of the working-class circles in which anarchists organized, and beyond the readership of their periodicals, the renown of anarchists was more closely associated with singular, sensationalized acts of violence. After the events

---

14   Ibid., 746.
15   Mauro Stampacchia, *"L'anarchismo umanista e mondialista di Pietro Gori"* (Lecture given at the Palazzo Granducale, Livorno, Italy, 2008).

Nitti mentioned, which all took place outside of Italy, no better example could be provided than that of Gaetano Bresci (1869–1901), an Italian who had immigrated to the United States, where he made a living as a weaver while contributing to anarchist journals in New Jersey. Bresci was disgusted after reading news of the massacre ordered by the second King of Italy, Umberto I, of about a hundred demonstrators protesting high bread prices in Milan in 1898. The King went so far as to decorate the general responsible for ordering his troops to fire upon the unarmed protestors. Calling in his debts from all his friends, Bresci bought a ticket back to Italy, where he shot the king dead in Monza in 1900, apparently acting upon his own initiative.

The Bresci regicide was a source of contention within the anarchist community. As evidenced by the flurry of reaction pieces sent in to newspapers, many condoned his action: the king, aside from his callous disregard for the lives of his subject, was a symbol of political power, monarchy, authority, all tools of oppression devoid of legitimacy from an anarchist point of view. If Umberto I thought it was alright to order the death of his unarmed subjects, how could a simple switching of roles be morally reprehensible?

Yet a fair number of anarchists also adhered to antimilitarism, a perspective that ranges from condemnation of the state's monopoly over violence to general pacifism. In her pamphlets illustrating the coercive and destructive effects of the army on lower-class families, Leda adhered to an antimilitarism very similar to the philosophy expounded by her socialist friend Ezio Bartalini (1884–1962). Bartalini founded the first Italian anti-militarist periodical *Peace* (*La Pace*) in 1903, and made his name know by publishing and lecturing extensively on how war was yet another mechanism of class oppression, as one state sends its proletariat to fight the proletariat of another country while those at the top of the socioeconomic food chain enjoy the spoils. Indeed, to a propagandist, the best weapons for social revolution were words, as Leda explained her chosen vocation:

> [...] I have always had faith in the value of creating propa-
> ganda for our ideas—whether through the press or through
> speech, leaving it to the more important people, who are
> better educated and more esteemed, to write the books, to
> expound upon theories, to outline paths to follow—in hopes

of continuing the mission to help those who don't know us or our ideas to understand the value of the Ideas we advocate. The propaganda of every faith, of every thought, of every ideal is an almost instinctive need for every thinking being, and is essentially a form of protest against the imposition of laws, habits, "obligations" that work against people who see things differently and generally have different points of view on human affairs. It is inside of us, in our thoughts; the hope that these things will materialize one day in the future. It is natural to express this hope, to present it as a possible form of moral revenge, it is natural to want to sow it in fertile soil. It is true that many seeds are scattered and lost in the field of uncultivated minds, but someone who believes in the value of propaganda does not give up trying.

An Individualist Anarchist with an avid mind dedicated to contradicting everything, a deconstructive critic with a vast knowledge of theoretical works to discuss and ponder, informed me of his rather disconcerting opinion on the work of propagandists, a craft I'd say I have instinctively practiced since early adolescence. He wrote: "I don't believe propaganda has any value for the masses of sheep, stuffed with old and new lies, servile slaves with gregarious habits: they cannot be convinced and will remain what they already are. I, however, write for my moral satisfaction, to defend my ideas and attack the ideas everyone else accepts. As well as for the few people who are able to understand me."

Well, in my opinion he seems to be doing the same thing I am: with the simple propaganda of anarchist ideas, rendered clear and accessible to brains gifted with intelligence and receptive to the desire for freedom. Herein lies the difference: he, emphasizing his vast, deep knowledge, nourished on the works of the masters of the "superman" theory—Stirner, Nietzsche, and other writers—directs his propaganda to the scholars, to the "initiated," while the propagandists, who are, let's say, more common, reach out to those who are unaware, to those who do not yet understand the magnitude, the truth of anarchist Ideas. The propagandists do not consider it below themselves to speak to the humans who struggle, who suffer,

who weakly submit to the crooked commands of governments, who even consent to die in Wars desired by their own
enemies, because they do not understand the moral greatness
of revolt, the singular beauty of rebellion. It is not true that
nobody understands, that everyone remains oppressed by
their unconscious cowardice. I have the personal experience
of knowing that I have enlightened many people obfuscated
by fear and weakened by the slavery imposed upon them
through the laws of this liberticidal society. Direct action,
violent rebellion, the necessary role models who stand up to
the tyranny that prevails in every era, in every Nation, ordered
by the despots in control; these have always been embodied
by Men who certainly didn't believe themselves to be "super-
men." Just think of Gaetano Bresci. And rather than explain
pages written by the great writers or discuss the theories of
thinkers from the past, someone who does not possess this
level of culture can very well, as I see it, dedicate themselves
to simple propaganda, to try, at least to try, to free humanity
from the symbolic shackles that the State, the Church—and
today this phantasmagoric institution of "Science"—place as
insurmountable barriers along the path of human development. It is true: some people are quick to condemn this poor
human race, which we are all a part of. But I know that this
sort of contempt for the resignation, the cowardice of the
masses, is actually provoked by observing how individuals are
subjected to every form of tyranny disguised as patriotism,
religion, civil duty, without daring to rebel. Underneath this
harsh criticism, this bitter language, there is always—among
those with Anarchist convictions—a noble heart and an
excessively strong feeling, so extreme it would welcome a
catastrophe that could sweep away from this the Earth—already so tortured!—the monstrous form of "civilization" that
sows wars while singing hymns to Peace, that throws billions
into works of destruction, contrived by the insane brains of
the so-called atomic "scientists," that accumulates power for
dominating entities in Parliaments and Ministries, that raises
altars to men worthy only of being thrown off their pedestals
of ambition and deranged criminality.

[…] Our simple propaganda always expresses, to whomever, our thoughts and our aversion to all of the evil that a few individuals cause to the detriment of millions of beings. We don't need to be superhuman in order to produce this propaganda. We just need to be Anarchists.

In one of our magazines edited in Milan, Giuseppe Monanni—a confirmed and active individualist who, like me, had to work since the age of thirteen and could not attend school—wrote: "We studied on the Work benches, and we graduated as human beings." And I believe the vast majority of propagandists could also tell a similar story.

[…] I could have written a graduate thesis on the works of Friedrich Nietzsche since, while proofreading the drafts of eleven volumes released by the Casa Editrice Monanni, I read every single volume a good four times, and I know the German Philosopher almost by heart, as well as Stirner's *The Ego and Its Own* and *Minor Writings*. But my female mind was better able to learn the value of anarchist Ideas from the likes of Luigi Molinari, Pietro Gori, Ezio Bartalini, Errico Malatesta, and many others who are "one of us," so close to us, who shared our fate through all of the struggles that we have experienced and overcome. To speak while remembering their voices, to follow the example of their lives, I think propaganda proves useful against the ignorance that dominates, against the bad faith that wins through the cowardice of those who fear going against the current. And going against the current has always been the volition of those who, accepting libertarian Ideas, against all enemies great and small, strive to be "faithful till the end."[16]

Over the decades, Leda matured as a writer, transitioning from publishing her propaganda in short pamphlets and articles to fleshing out her political ideas into full-length, pulpy novels. A fan of Tolstoy, she no doubt understood the merits of literature that combined political passions with a focus on how social dynamics and power relations affected the lives of individuals. She adopted a variety of pseudonyms—Djali,

---

16   Leda Rafanelli, *La Propaganda*, (unpublished manuscript, date unknown), 1–4. Fondo "LR-M" conserved at the ABC.

Zagura Sicula, Bruna, Costantino Bazaroff, Adamo, Ida Paoli, Nada, Sahara—some for fun, and some to protect herself from state censors. The majority of her newspaper contributions she kept copies of in her papers, however, are signed in her own name.

Her first novel, *A Dream of Love* (*Un Sogno d'Amore*) was published in 1904 by the Rafanelli-Polli publishing house and narrates the adventures of two sisters, one of whom is "in love with political ideas," who set out to explore free love and sensual pleasure. *New Seed* (*Seme Nuovo*), published in 1912, continues the focus on young women exploring free love as it follows the story of Vera, who is in the midst of developing her anarchist consciousness. *The Hero of the Masses* represents the culmination of Leda's full-length, propagandistic fiction for young Italian audiences. Although she would continue to write a dozen or so more novels after its publication in 1920, her focus shifted to other, more psychologically complex issues.

***

The animal had torn free from its rope, liberating itself in its agony. Hearing the door open it rushed toward the opening only to pause, stunned, on the threshold illuminated by the white glare of the full moon. It let out a loud moo. The boys didn't need to show it where the grass was, and the cow escaped, while its little calf, which hadn't been tied up, followed.

Finally free, the cow jumped over a small ditch and stopped in a field of wheat, with the little one at its side. It dove its greedy nostrils into the fresh wave of future bread for humans and began eating. The calf tried eating, tearing at the blades, struggling to chew, confounding its exhaustion, moistening its dry throat. The two boys, who had stayed behind the two starving animals, watched them, happy to hear the gurgling noises of their avid chewing. They held hands and spoke in low voices, forgetting about going back home.

"If I had known she had gotten free from her rope I would have thrown her grass through the bars. How are we going to get her to go back into the stall now?"

"Mister Andrea will take care of it."

"She's eating all of the wheat...Maybe opening the door was a mistake."

Meanwhile, Lorenzo thought of how surprised the landowners would be if the workers decided to get revenge by opening all of the stall doors tonight, before the soldiers arrived. The bourgeoisie, the rich landlords had no other religion but their own *interests*, no other God than money. That's what his Master at the forge always said. And couldn't he, a boy, teach them a well-deserved lesson if he opened the doors to the other stalls? It wasn't right for innocent animals to die of hunger. And true, they would eat the grass and the grain, ruining everything. But were those same landowners thinking of the children from poor families who suffered from hunger, now that their fathers were on strike?

Lorenzo continued thinking, unaware that his action was anticipating a future theory used in social struggles. He decided to open all of the stalls, to set the hungry animals free, let them reign over the fields that would be invaded by the soldiers controlled by the landlords in the morning. Nino, scared and worried, nevertheless admired his boldness.

Lorenzo then went from stall to stall, opening as many as he could, using his tools and his dexterity. By the time he got to the third stall he already knew what to do in order to avoid getting rushed by the animals, full of momentum and already free from the ropes they had torn in their fury of vain anticipation. As soon as the lock gave way, the boys slowly opened the door and threw in armfuls of grain and grass, which Nino had been gathering as Lorenzo broke the simple locks with his tools. Most stalls were only closed by latches. The dogs stopped barking when they saw the two boys, their friends. The dogs had been barking quite a bit lately during the nights of the strike, with the carabinieri making the rounds and the strikers looking out for strikebreakers. Yet dawn was approaching and everyone was resting, people and guard dogs.

Meanwhile, the farm animals descended upon the precious food, devouring it greedily, fighting over it. Using their muzzles, they pushed the doors wide open and lunged outside with triumphant, deep lows. But the fragrance of the fresh grass immediately delighted the parched mouths of the starving animals, and they made their way through the cultivated fields, panting at the abundant feast.

The countryside was soon populated with free beasts: it was as if a horde of vandals had set upon those fields in order to destroy them.

A herd of horses galloped their way to freedom out of a rich man's unattended stable, the wind in their manes and their eyes full of madness as they rushed to assist with the devastation. Lorenzo and the young boy, satisfied and content, slipped through the hedges to return home unobserved. They had gone rather far, and thought about the surprise waiting for everyone in the morning. The soldiers would have to hunt down the runaway animals, in addition to mowing the grass and cleaning up the stalls! And they laughed, running barefoot between clumps of earth, tired and sleepy, like shadowy phantoms in the transparent semi-darkness that comes right before the break of day.

But the farms were already on *alert*. The cries of the freed animals heard from nearby had woken up a few sleeping people, who soon understood that the stalls had been opened. The first to rise from his bed was a stout rancher, who wondered how his meek little goats had been able to force open the stall door. But just as he opened the window, taking aim with his rifle, he stifled an exclamation of astonishment and dismay. What in the world had happened?

Under the glow of the moon, which bathed the entire countryside in opaque light, highlighting the flat fields amid the dark shadows of the wide valleys, the light-colored plots where the wheat was planted took on a green glint. And in that sea of grass, the black shapes of the animals moved about, resting, raising their enormous heads with bellows of joy. Satiated cows plunged their white muzzles in the fresh grain tender with dew as black bulls continued devouring it, insatiable and voracious. Suddenly an excited horse, with long blades of grass hanging out from the sides of its mouth, darted off, free from bits and saddles, weaving between the other lazy and dim-witted animals in a configuration that seemed like a ballroom dance.

Then the alarm was given, and bewildered men rushed out armed and furious, cursing the slaughter of the growing wheat. Every window lit up, doors opened, and human voices, hoarse with sleep, resonant with surprise, high with anger, mixed in with the bellows of the animals. And then a wild nighttime chase took place, through the devastated fields, under the fading glare of the beautiful, round, setting moon. The scene was unusual, something new. The horses scattered, trampling the budding fields, soaring over the bordering hedges with all of the momentum their heels could muster. And from afar, it seemed like they were taunting their chasers, resting their shivering backs and nervous legs for brief intervals before starting to run again and escape even further away, grabbing yet another mouthful of grass as if out of spite.

But the devastation, and the actual extent of the vandalism, only came to light when the radiant dawn brightened the sky over the black pine forest. The soldiers arrived too late. The strikers had gotten their revenge in advance. Yet none of the tenant farmers, and not even the strikers themselves, knew or even suspected that all of this havoc was the work of two young boys who had nothing to do with any union, who had no idea who Sabot was, who had never even heard of his name. The act of *sabotage* had been performed without premeditation, and turned out to be successful only by chance.[17]

***

Leda's activity did not go unnoticed by government authorities. In 1907, she was charged by the Prefecture of Florence for incitement after several of her antimilitarist pamphlets were sequestered, but was released from the charges under an amnesty.[18] She would be kept under state surveillance over the next two decades, yet despite periodic raids and sequestrations of her material, was never imprisoned or pushed into exile, like many of her compagni.

17 Leda Rafanelli, *L'Eroe della Folla*, 39–44.
18 Alberto Ciampi, *Leda Rafanelli—Carlo Carrà, Un Romanzo: Arte e Politica in un Incontro Ormai Celebre*, 33.

CHAPTER IV
Free Love and Feminility

Why thank you, my lady, for giving me so much satisfaction that I couldn't help but smirk with an exquisite sense of irony as you shook my hand.

And do you know why now, at this quiet hour of the night, I'm wasting my time writing to you? It's because I want to tell you the truth that you fail to see, the truth you perhaps won't really understand. And I'm writing this without any *premeditated* objective. I certainly don't expect to *persuade* you to support my ideas: it's just an amusing way to pass the time.

Anyhow I'd like to start off by shocking you with an explanation for my little smirk, just a tad scornful. I was sneering at you because I could guess what was going on in your little head as you looked at me, thinking the exact opposite of what was passing through my mind. You think that you're envied, but in reality, I pity you!

Perhaps you won't believe me, but that's how it is. I feel sorry for you and your lovely yet empty bourgeois existence. You were telling me, ever so effusively, how happy you were (although our association is much too superficial to merit your trust) so that I would envy you, overcome with the desire to possess your fortune, as you prattled on with carefully studied nonchalance about your luxuries and leisures.

You told me about your *brilliant* life, about the last gift you received for your name day, of the high position your husband holds; just so I—and perhaps this is what you thought you could read in my eyes—would think: "How nice it would be if I could have her life!"

You weren't trying to inspire my jealousy out of cruelty; rather, you wanted me to compare our lives to the lives led by bourgeois women, so that I (and I think you vaguely understand what I'm talking about) would *spring into action*, saying: "One day we, the women of the proletariat, will also leave the working world to spend our time thinking about clothes and trying on hats. One day we'll finally be able to decorate ourselves with shiny earrings and necklaces and rings—we'll finally be able to waste our days in front of the mirror, trying to make our faces even more beautiful and attractive, using art to correct the errors of nature."

But here, my dear lady, is where you're wrong. To us proletariat women, intelligent women with subversive ideas in our heads, none of this matters at all. We prefer to be *women*, not *females*. We don't want, nor do we admire the things your life is made of.

You bourgeois women only have one objective: to use your beauty to attract others. You don't bother to cultivate your mind, your thoughts, or your heart. When you grow older, you'll see yourself lose your power, yet still deluded with pleasure, you'll try to remain beautiful, you'll paint yourself and make a fool of yourself. And the memories of your former youth will be devoid of any days, or even hours during which you truly and intensely *lived*.

Because, when you think about it, no life is emptier than a *brilliant* life. That type of life seems to be full of passion and adventure, but deep down it's devoid of anything real, or anything deeply felt—and this is for one reason and one reason only: *high society* women must employ the most refined form of coquetry.

Yet we subversive women have much more respect for a prostitute than a *coquette*. The prostitute sells herself and atones for her prostitution by wearing it like a mark on her forehead. The *coquette* inflames passion and fuels desire without ever following through; people adore her and she does not love them; she makes a thousand promises and gives nothing; a hundred handsome men court her and then, finally, she settles down with an ugly old man, only because he has lots of *money*.

That's all it's about, money! That's what you bourgeois women aspire to. You love money and money alone: it's what you use to satisfy all of your whims, all of your desires for luxury and waste. It's wretched to be able to *buy* everything you want! You'll never feel the satisfaction of the conquest, the satisfaction of having wanted, of succeeding in getting something through your own strength and willpower.

Why should we envy you? For your beauty? It's too deceptive, it's like a greenhouse flower, it can't stand up to a gust of wind. For your knowledge? It's superficial. For your luxury, your elegant and fashionable clothes? *Fashion* is a *science* that seems rather ridiculous to us. For your lovers? Hardly! Those affairs are merely flings complicated by extravagant ideas of romance or stupid sentimentality: we, on the other hand, love as nature intends us to.

So now what? You don't even have faith, while we have ideas. You're not even like a religious peasant who, as ignorant and stupid as she might be, is still a fervent believer. You are religious because you know that the clergy sustains your social class. You go to mass at noon so you don't have to get up early, and you show off your meticulous grooming at church as if it were the theater, criticizing your friends and starting fickle little romances. Once I saw a peasant woman fall to her knees in the mud to show her humility as a religious procession passed by, while at the same time a lady looked for a clean-swept doorstep so that she could kneel without ruining her silk dress. While the ignorance of the religious peasant bothered me, I couldn't help but note the stark moral contrast between these two actions.

You bourgeois women always act this way: your comfort and convenience guide every thought that passes through your head. And you think that you are *righteous* people. Your morals—oh please, let's not even talk about them!

And now, after reading this little *diatribe*, you, Madame, probably wonder why, then, we subversive people are demanding equality. If we don't envy you in the least, we should just leave things as they are, right? But no, that would be another error. We know that while one class squanders away

in luxury, the other class, which achieves whatever luxury
it has through work, suffers from the cold, hunger, distress,
and fatigue. We know that for every one hundred bourgeois
women wearing silk garments, thousands of proletariat wom-
en fall ill with tuberculosis in the spinning mills; we know
that behind the opaque splendor of every little pearl on your
necklaces looms the gloomy shadow of an indigenous diver
who died while harvesting oysters along the faraway coasts of
India. Your gold bracelets were once bathed with the sweat
and blood of miners who descended into the bowels of the
earth to extract precious metals from the rocks. Everything,
basically, that serves and pleases you is our blood, pain, hunger and sweat. We cry for freedom and equality. But it's not
because we aspire to lead a life as useless as yours, but because
the masses in revolt wish to achieve the well-being guaranteed
by the natural laws of life.[1]

***

It seems logical to assume that Leda was a feminist, yet as autonomous as
she was in her choices—particularly concerning her unique approach to
family and romantic partnerships—she never claimed to be a feminist,
and ultimately took a stand *against* erasing the divisions between men
and women, offering her own ideas as to how exactly those divisions
could be conceptualized. It is difficult to summarize, or even coherently
trace, how her thoughts on women's issues developed over her ninety
one years.

As evidenced in the essay above, "To a bourgeois lady" ("Ad una signora borghese"), Leda did not hold back from attacking bourgeois women
for what she considered an impoverished approach to living, superficiality, and class smugness. However, she did not spare working women from
criticism either, particularly regarding their insouciant reproduction of
oppressive social systems. Leda advocated for the liberation of women
just as she advocated for the liberation of men, particularly as regards free
love; yet given the state of the Italian feminist movement(s) in the early

---

1   Leda Rafanelli, "Ad una signora borghese," in *Per l'idea nostra: Raccolta di ar-
     ticoli e bozzetti di propaganda* (Florence: Libreria Rafanelli-Polli E C., 1905),
     85–90. Fondo "LR-M" conserved at the ABC.

twentieth century, not to mention her individualist approach to anarchism, she never identified with any current of feminism. Free from any specific affiliation or adherence to a finite form of feminism, Leda instead spent her energy exploring the question of what, at heart, femininity was, and what a liberated woman might make of her femininity in a world in which the old social constructs no longer apply.

Feminism as we understand it today—as a part of a larger field of inquiry that also delves into the issues of sexual orientation and identities—is much different than how it was when it got started in Europe and North America in the late nineteenth century. Generally recognized as inferior to men in the eyes of the law, Italian women were unable to vote and prohibited from holding any type of public office. Losing most rights upon marriage, women were given harsh punishments for committing adultery—even if the incident took place before marriage—while men would only be reprimanded if they kept their concubine on family property. Although not formally sanctioned by the law, honor killings were common in cases in which an unmarried woman's virginity was compromised; yet the family name could be saved through a reparative marriage, thus a woman might be forced to take her rapist as a husband as a conciliatory measure. Under the 1865 Pisanelli Code, the public school system provided education to both girls and boys, yet, given the fact it was still commonly considered that the best education for girls was no education whatsoever, many families decided to keep their daughters out of school, lest their morality be threatened.[2]

Alongside the industrial revolution, feminism developed later in Italy than it had in France or England. There was no united front for female emancipation: class divisions drove a line between "bourgeois" feminism, focused on suffrage and women's entry into public life, and socialist feminism, which called for gender equality within an entirely new society. Between these two camps many women worked toward improving education, healthcare, labor conditions, and legal rights for women. The Catholic church, particularly wary of its authority being sapped by the newly born Italian state, not to mention the rise of secular scientific culture throughout Europe, began to recognize women as powerful agents of religious education, thus paving the way for a Christian feminist movement that, in many respects, was rather subversive to feminist causes.

---

2   Perry Wilson, *Italiane: Biografia del Novecento*, 8–25.

Echoing her disdain for the bourgeoisie, Leda pronounced that the emancipation of women was not, in her opinion, going to be ushered in by the feminist movement:

> [Feminism] is the fruit of today's society, and therefore, from my point of view, fruit without any good substance and full of poison (...) While the proletarian woman more or less energetically combats the oppressor, the bourgeois woman (...) also rises up. But against whom? Against men; against males. Yes, the bourgeois woman has only one issue; and feminism has only one purpose: to reach the same level as man in his studies; imitate him in the professional world; to be compared as equals. Unfortunately this makes her seem ridiculous. (...) Perhaps the bourgeois woman will see men as the obstacle to her ideas and will fight against them, as it's certainly easier to fight against males than it is to fight against society as a whole (...) feminism is a poisonous fruit of modern society, that strives to do nothing else but create female attorneys; who, just like male attorneys, will be perfectly useless in the society of the future, as soon as we, the people, render laws and courts useless and therefore eliminate them.[3]

Leda thus depicts feminism as a bourgeois ideology focused on increasing women's participation in the institutions she, as an anarchist, did not consider legitimate. Indeed, suffrage was high on the list of priorities of feminist pioneers such as Anna Maria Mozzoni (1837–1920), who published the book *Woman and Her Social Relationships* (*La donna e i suoi rapporti sociali*) in 1864, detailing an eighteen-point plan that included a variety of legal, educational, and social reforms in order to improve gender equality in the eyes of the law and through participation in the public sphere.[4] Mozzoni was born into a family with noble origins, yet her perspective was not necessarily shared by the majority of women

---

3   Leda Rafanelli, "Il Feminismo" *Il Pensiero*, Year II, number 17–18, 16 September 1904. Cited in Ciampi, Alberto (editor), *Leda Rafanelli—Carlo Carrà, Un Romanzo: Arte e Politica in un Incontro Ormai Celebre* (Venice: Centro Internazionale della Grafica, 2005), 30.

4   Emilia Sarogni, *La donna Italiana. Il lungo cammino verso I diritti 1861–1994* (Parma: Pratiche Editrice, 1995), 28–29.

in the upper and growing middle classes. Instead of looking for the root causes of their oppression in the society that surrounded them, women of the petite bourgeoisie were more likely to focus on climbing the social and economic ladder through strategic marriages.[5] This was the mentality that Leda deconstructed in "To a bourgeois lady" and regularly ridiculed in other pamphlets and short stories.[6] She was somewhat less vehement in her critiques of the type of feminism Mozzoni advocated, as she was in general rather sympathetic to the socialist perspective.

When the socialist party was founded in 1892, the majority of factory workers were women. By 1900, estimates stated that between thirty and forty percent of all Italian women worked for wages: the figures are unclear due to ambiguities regarding how to categorize part-time work and labor performed at home, as was commonly the case in the textile industry. Women were considered to be more docile and obedient and therefore willing to work for longer hours and lower wages than men.[7] The socialist movement could not ignore the potential and the significance of this demographic. Yet, at heart, the socialist movement was imminently concerned with overturning the capitalist order, and considered the question of women's rights to be, at best, of secondary importance.

In a 1901 pamphlet entitled *Feminism and Socialism*, socialist Ernesta Campolonghi wrote: "Women, in my opinion, will only be equal to men when all men are equal amongst themselves; women will be free and independent from men only when men are free and independent amongst themselves; when society is created in such a way that all work according to their strengths and receive adequate compensation for their own work. Equality is a word with no basis in reality. How can a woman be equal to a man today, if it's the man who earns money and takes care of her?"[8] Since the schism with Marx in the 1870s, however, anti-authoritarian critics of Italian socialism consistently maintained that any

---

5   Joyce Lussu, *Padre, Padrone, Padreterno: Breve storia di schiave e matrone, villane e castellane, streghe e mercantesse, proletarie e padrone* (Milan: Gabriele Mazzotta Editore, 1976), 82.

6   "Due Vittime" in Leda Rafanelli, *Donne e Femmine* (Milan: Casa Editrice Sociale, 1922).

7   Perry Wilson, *Italiane: Biografia del Novecento*, 27–29.

8   Ernesta Campolonghi, *Femminismo e Socialismo* (Savona: Tipografia Ligura, 1901), 12. There is little biographical data available on Ernesta Campolonghi; however, given the fact that her husband Luigi lived from 1876–1944, she likely lived within a similar time span.

socialist government of the future could potentially institute its own oppressive hierarchy, in which women might not be any better off than they were under capitalism.

Anna Kuliscioff (1857–1925), one of the first female doctors in Italy, is alternately defined as a socialist feminist and an anarcho-feminist: in reality, she participated in a variety of movements and considered the socialist party to be the most convenient vehicle for improving the lot of working class women, whom she served through her medical practice, thus earning her the nickname "doctor of the poor" (dottora dei poveri).[9] It was not her socialist affiliation but her participation in a pro-Falasha solidarity campaign during WWI that led her and Leda to meet for the first time.[10] Through her writing, participation in conferences, and organizing activities, Kuliscioff focused specifically on women's issues, including health and labor conditions at the workplace, protection of women and children from exploitative conditions, institution of maternity benefits and, eventually, suffrage. She advocated that the transformation of society would also entail a transformation of family and personal relations, issues that were not commonly addressed in socialist rhetoric.[11]

Socialism, however, was not the biggest pull among working class women. Particularly interesting in the Italian context is the role the Catholic church played in encouraging women to become active in religious associations and movements during the early twentieth century, essentially sanctioning their participation in public life, previously considered to be a sphere reserved for men.

Promoting women's social integration through involvement in the church was seen as a means of defense against the growing power of secular forces in Italy—namely, the new national government as well as the growing associationism amongst the working classes. The 1891 Rerum Novarum encyclical specifically addressed the labor and social conditions of the working class, paving the way for "social catholicism" and the mobilization of women, considered the more devoted and reliable of the two sexes, to fend off the moral threats of modernity, particularly rising

9   Miguel Malagreca, "Lottiamo Ancora: Reviewing One Hundred and Fifty Years of Italian Feminism," *Journal of International Women's Studies,* Vol. 7 #4 2006, 71.

10   Pier Carlo Masini, Introduction to Leda Rafanelli, *Una Donna e Mussolini,* 21.

11   Emilia Sarogni, *La donna Italiana. Il lungo cammino verso I diritti 1861–1994* (Parma: Pratiche Editrice, 1995), 116–117.

atheism among men.[12] "Catholic feminism" did not seek to establish new rights for women: rather, it instituted new duties for women as the agents of religious education, particularly within the family unit.

Italian women generally identified with the Catholic religion, and the lure of Catholic women's associations was anchored in the idea that offering women the possibility to participate in church social activities—even if still at an unequal or even lower status—would satisfy their "modest" desires for inclusion.[13] Under this logic, local associations, magazines, and federations were formed, sometimes exclusively for women and at other times for both sexes, in either case bringing women together to effect a spiritual regeneration, largely through philanthropic activity. Adelaide Coari (1881–1966), a prominent figure in the field of Catholic feminism, reflected the spirit of the movement in writing: "When I think that men no longer respect all that is religious, and that the name of Christ and his doctrine has been removed from our schools and public institutions, I tremblingly wonder if women are not to blame for this, as women are too small-minded with their ideas and weak in the presence of evil."[14]

Like any other version of feminism at the time, however, Catholic feminists held divergent points of view and agendas: they generally agreed that public education needed to be improved and legal advances made for women, but that seemed to be the limit of any sort of common platform. Other issues, such as suffrage and labor rights, or even the right to labor outside of the family household, remained contentious within this group.

***

The human simplicity of our theories clearly demonstrates how absurd legal complications affecting families paralyze the flame of feelings, of love, of affection, which should be at the base of the family itself. Therefore, there's no reason why everyday women would want to preserve these coercive and anti-natural forms of the free union of the sexes. Happiness, which people

---

12 Perry Wilson, *Italiane: Biografia del Novecento*, 56.
13 Lucetta Scaraffia and Anna Maria Isastia, *Donne ottimiste: femminismo e associazioni borghesi nell'Otto e Novecento* (Bologna: Il Mulino, 2002), 111.
14 Ibid., 92.

today seek in vain through wearisome and thoughtless false-hoods of feelings and affections, would actually be more prev-alent among a free people, among individuals who are masters of their own lives as well as their own thoughts.

This applies to the family as well as to love. But another *fear* divides and distances women from our revolutionary pro-paganda. We are *atheists*, we negate the truth of every religion, and this positive negation offends everyone who, even if they don't have a rudimentary *faith*, accept *religion* because they *were born to that religion and must die under that religion*.

This is moronic reasoning: even if lies and falsehood man-aged to fog up someone's brain when they were not yet strong enough to think for themselves, to understand how to create their own ideas, it's no justification for continuing to enslave our minds to serve these dogmas, which we are told represent the supreme truth and yet are so…mysterious and inexplica-ble, as…God would have it.

However, in many pamphlets dedicated to women—some written in good faith and other times a product of the shrewd opportunism of petty politicians who don't want to alienate the masses—you'll read that *the question of religion is a private, intimate, personal issue*, and therefore, in a new society, every individual would be free to believe what they deem to be true.

Which is fine. Yet this point of view, however faithful to the principle of individual freedom, shouldn't stop us from clearly explaining the ideas behind our propaganda.

It's time that we explain to our women, once and for all, that *our positive ideas are based on atheism and materialism*, as we are convinced that all religions are nothing more than lies and scams hypocritically hidden under fables and mysticism.

If something cannot be explained, it is absurd. Anything hidden under veils of *impenetrable mysteries* can never be accepted.

Any kind of faith in a supernatural power cannot coexist with the powerful thoughts of a free man. It cannot be toler-ated alongside the revolutionary ideas we advocate. We believe only in the work of creation that is life, since we can see with our own eyes the creative force at work every hour, every minute, busily and mightily. Unfortunately humans, nature's most beautiful work, even though they possesses all sorts of material and intellectual energies, create dogma, bow down to laws, enchain themselves to others just like themselves, stopping the march of progress towards a future of freedom.

What can we say about *priests?* It goes without saying that we fight against everything they do, all that they believe with all of their doctrine. Priests are the ministers of a religion we don't recognize, and as for us, we don't want *clergy* for humans or for our free theory. Ideas are not dogma, because our ideas do not form a religion that will be imposed upon others in the future.

Our ideas are something higher, bigger, mightier. We believe in the total freedom of the individual in the united international of people who are free from all chains. We are the ones who must destroy these oppressive chains, break them, twist them, in the compelling struggle to reclaim our rights. And our women must help us in this task: more oppressed than males in this liberticidal society, they must therefore fight with even more energy and courage. Onwards![15]

***

"To Eve the Slave (Religion)" was reworked by Leda several times as a pamphlet and later as an essay, providing a clear and intrinsically anarchist critique of religion directed specifically to women. Of course, this essay reeks of hypocrisy, given the fact that Leda began identifying herself as a member of the Muslim faith in the very first years of the twentieth century. There is no easy way to reconcile her simultaneous criticism of organized religion and her own practice of Islam: she refers to Islam, too, as a religion, rather than a spirituality or moral code.

Leda produced two sequel pamphlets on this theme: *To Eve the Slave (Family and Love)* and *To Eve the Slave (The Future Society),* both focused on women's conservatism and fear of change. She argued that resistance to revolutionary ideas sprung from ill-placed loyalties to structures of

---

15   Leda Rafanelli, "A l'Eva schiava (religione)," in *Per l'idea nostra: Raccolta di articoli e bozzetti di propaganda* (Florence: Libreria Rafanelli-Polli E C., 1905), 62–66. Fondo "LR-M" conserved at the ABC.

the current society—the family and the nation, respectively—founded on principles of convenience and slavery. She called upon women to see beyond the contradictions and falsehoods of the "moral" society and to work toward the destruction of its institutions, essentially through understanding and putting their faith in the concept of free love, as is the particular case of *To Eve the Slave (Family and Love)*.

Leda's output on women's issues was not limited to inflammatory propaganda: she wrote several coming-of-age novels featuring fiery female protagonists who set out to rebel against social constraints and explore their freedom, often in anarchist circles. Leda's 1912 novel, *New Seed (Seme Nuovo)*, was built upon a literary narrative that combined youthful romance with the discovery of political passion, a device used successfully in her first novel, *A Dream of Love (Un Sogno di Amore)*, published in 1905 and later translated into Spanish. The plot of *New Seed* follows Vera, a young woman, as she navigates her way through strikes, meetings, rallies, trials: all in all, the everyday comings and goings of a young anarchist. Through Vera's eyes, the reader critiques the church, political oppression, school institutions, as well as some of Vera's fellow anarchists for their alcohol abuse, lack of consistency between theory and practice, and naïve ferocity. The narrative also follows her romantic affairs within her explorations of free love, presented as the only way an anarchist can truly love. Vera is a positive hero, a role model, an example in politics and relationships for young women seeking to live anarchically.

Throughout the decades, Leda's writings on women drifted away from propaganda and instructional novels and took on a more reflective, inward-looking dimension. Leda published *Like a Meteor (Come una meteora)* in 1926: rather than present new role models, the novel provides a long and detailed study of the superficiality of the bourgeois world in which women are consumed with appearances, flirtations, and superficiality. However, unlike the quick and scathing essays she had written denouncing bourgeois values in decades prior, *Like a Meteor* takes on a slightly melancholy flavor as the reader begins to sympathize with the protagonist, upper-class Amina, understanding that her empty existence was forced upon her by her position in a restrictive society, not by her own choice or volition. Leda never let up on her criticism of women's blind acceptance of authority, yet seems to have grown more understanding, given women's lack of an obvious or easy alternative, not to mention the threat of social isolation.

Her 1922 collection of short stories, *Women and Females* (*Donne e femmine*), is, perhaps, the most difficult of all of Leda's work to analyze. The title itself presents a challenge: what exactly is the difference between a woman and a female? The connotations Leda personally grants to these terms apparently changed over the years as well: while she proclaims loudly that "We prefer to be *women*, not *females*" in "To a Bourgeois Lady," she later writes in an unpublished manuscript: "I have been and am only a female. And as a female only love and motherhood give value to my life."[16]

It would be easy to simply dismiss this discrepancy as a sign that Leda had changed her mind or that her understanding of femininity had developed in a different direction over the years. And while there is no doubt that her ideas did change with time, as with anyone who does not subscribe to dogma, there is nevertheless a great deal of value in exploring the possible dichotomies presented through the interplay of the terms "woman" and "female." Through growing recognition of transexuality, even the discipline of anatomy now fails to provide one valid definition of what a woman, or a female, is. Yet we have nothing to lose in musing on the various options.

Perusing through dictionaries, the difference between "woman" and "female" takes on a slight biological undertone: women are adult human creatures, and females are any animal or plant that produces eggs. Extending this categorization to the literary sphere, a "woman" could be understood to be a whole, dynamic person; while a "female" is the role played to complement the "male" role specifically as regards reproduction or sexuality. In a sense, a woman could take on a variety of roles at different times and in different situations—including the female role—while the female role has its limits and is defined almost entirely by its contrast to the male role. Indeed, as Leda experiments with the juxtapositions between "woman" and "female" in her writing, she also contrasts "man" and "male"; yet in neither case is the comparison explained nor consistently implemented in a way that would allow us to deduce one, specific meaning.

Yet in declaring herself as a female, and only a female, Leda is flirting with her readers. Her decades of political activism and enormous literary output were as much defining elements of her character as her

---

16 Leda Rafanelli, *Una donna e 4 uomini dell'oriente* (unpublished manuscript, date unknown). Conserved in a private collection owned and kindly made available by Fiamma Chessa.

motherhood and love affairs, and she was undoubtedly aware of this. Looking through her work, she tends to use the term "female" in describing intimate experiences and feelings, while "woman" is used when her characters act in more public capacities. Vera, the heroine of *New Seed*, is described as "completely enslaved to her nature, a strong-minded woman of action when up against society, yet ready to turn into a female as soon as she's near a male."[17]

The female could be better understood as a representation of sensuality and sexuality, a more natural and spontaneous dimension that belongs to the private sphere: an intimate self Leda was able to more closely cultivate during the last few decades of her life, during which she lived in relative solitude. The woman, then, is the social entity, something that belongs to the public sphere ruled by logic and intellect as defined in a male-dominated society, a realm in which women are defined and treated as inferior. By contrast, the female is free from societal constructs: more primitive, perhaps, but on a par with the male, both subjected to the laws of nature, not pitted against one another in a power struggle.

Rather than refuse the inferior status imposed upon women by a patriarchal society, Leda seems to embrace it, as she argues for the superiority of men while describing the epistolary friendship she had with her *compagno* Carlo Molaschi: "If you compare two individuals, one man and one woman, who have both reached a level of intellectual, idealistic, and social superiority, the Man is always higher. That's how it was between Carlo and I. The proof is in the letters we used to write to one another: he wrote what he really felt; I, unconsciously, composed 'literature,' as a woman always embellishes things...."[18] The fact that she belongs to the female gender is treated as an "insurmountable obstacle,"[19] as she often writes how her female mind limits her in understanding complex theoretical arguments and debate.

Leda's views on the superiority of men (not males) may come as somewhat shocking, considering how erudite she herself was, yet bear in mind that the playing field for intellectual discourse in the early twentieth

---

17   Leda Rafanelli, *Seme nuovo*, (Milan: Societa Editoriale Milanese, 1912), 59. Fondo "LR-M" conserved at the ABC.

18   Leda Rafanelli, Excerpt from *Compagni*, (unpublished manuscript, date unknown). Fondo "LR-MM-MLF" conserved at the ABC.

19   Christiane Guidoni, "Leda Rafanelli: 'Donna e Femmina,'" 65, in *Chroniques italiennes*, n° 39–40, 1994.

century had been created almost entirely by men, for men. Accordingly, logic, intellect, ideology, and literature can be all considered to be social institutions that were also created by men, with their own subjective criteria for judging inferiority or superiority. Women had been historically excluded from the creation of, and participation in, these social institutions, and therefore it would seem difficult and perhaps even undesirable, moving forward into a future free from oppressive social institutions, for women to excel within these institutions once they were, finally, granted access. Proclaiming the inferiority of women might also have served as a means of recognizing the inevitable result of historical exclusion and oppression, a somewhat fatalistic perspective that does not preclude the hope of things changing in the future. In terms of power dynamics, however, inferiority does not necessarily justify subordination.

Some of her work even seeks to explore the essence of a welcome and different femininity:

> A woman—whose passions are motivated by just two impulses, love and motherhood—speaks more with her heart than with her brain. Scholars of pathology also say that she speaks with her uterus; and she does indeed. The uterus is also a living organ, much like the heart; and all in all the heart is the motor that makes the blood flow, while the uterus creates, protects, gives birth to the future human. Perhaps it is true, feminine human compassion comes from the uterus, because the most sympathetic people are women-mothers. But every one of our organs are sacred and vital, necessary, indispensable to our nature. A person who loves life loves themselves, and all of themselves.[20]

It's difficult to say whether these ideas—splitting a person into interior/exterior dimensions, acknowledging a woman's inferiority in society as inevitable, seeking to pinpoint what singular mechanisms operate within a woman—could be considered progressive. Her position seems dangerously similar to dominant ideologies of the time that sought to explain the "natural" inferiority of women through their anatomical and psychological mechanisms, though Leda would never have used her arguments to support further oppression or denial of freedoms to women. Given the fact

20 Leda Rafanelli, *Una Donna e Mussolini*, 160.

that Leda never clearly spelled out her views on womanhood in a coherent and focused manner, we are left analyzing bits and pieces, often contradictory, from a variety of fictive, political, and autobiographical contexts.

Thus, rather than discussing feminism or the lack thereof, it may be more appropriate to refer to Leda's views on female issues as *feminility*: an inquiry into what femininity or womanhood was, an exploration of the female essence beyond the social world of prescribed gender roles and relationships. Leda's intellectual prowess, her practice of free love, and her general rebellion against all social mores of her time are evident in her words and actions. Yet in rejecting the notion of gender equality, the dominant ideology among other female leftists, she faced an intellectual vacuum: if "equality" represented the negation of the female identity, what would the female identity look like in its full, liberated form? What exactly does a woman need to be fulfilled, as compared to a man? Her attempts to fill this vacuum, although by no means comprehensive, nor the main focus of her literary activity, are nevertheless thought-provoking.

Women and Females sketches portraits of women between their public and private dimensions, delving into their mentalities and questioning their decisions, whether made for social approval or for more sincere and heartfelt reasons. Likely modeled after people whom Leda knew personally, the roles these women take on—maternity, marriage, solitude—are shown to be steps in a continuous process of creation, the cultivation of femininity, for better or for worse. Exploring jealousy, lauding maternity, deploring underdeveloped souls, praising women of high intelligence and pitying the women whose upper-class marriages are similar to situations of prostitution, Leda highlights what she considers to be the universal, eternal characteristics of the feminine condition. A key factor of this is motherhood, something she considered to be a gift of love, not a duty to the state, church, or social institution of the family. In *Women and Females*, mothers are described as "scared females," the "Madonna of the house," and "sacred givers of life."[21]

Yet her musings on motherhood are second in importance, in this work and others, to her advocacy and illustration of free love. Free love, in its original ideological incarnation, had little to do with promiscuity. In a nutshell, it attempted to demonstrate how sexual and emotional union should be achieved outside of the oppressive restraints of economic and social control, chiefly channeled through the institution of

---

21   Christiane Guidoni, "Leda Rafanelli: 'Donna e Femmina,'" 67–68.

marriage. Leda herself wrote the foreword to the Casa Editrice Sociale's 1921 release of a translated version of *Free Love* (*L'amore libero*), originally published in 1898 by Charles Albert, a pseudonym used by the French anarchist Charles Daudet (1869–1957).

Albert's work argues that sincere expression of love, true autonomy of sexual experience from social conditioning, as well as an end to prostitution and gender-based discrimination, could be achieved only through the overthrow of a state-sponsored, class-based society. In introducing the work, Leda acknowledges that the concept of free love is poorly understood, yet the oppressive structures of families as well as toxic perceptions of sex—both based on concepts other than love—need to be overcome before human social dynamics can evolve further. Love, she affirms, survives on freedom, not the imposition of equal status within a corrupt system:

> Understanding life and living it serenely, happily, in a blossom of joy, in a constant and intense, full affirmation of love—giving life to healthy fruit, offering all of our brothers and sisters affectionate and constructive acceptance; understanding the inevitable pain, and remaining calm throughout mortal struggles, all with knowing awareness and a sense of peace: this is the human mission, and all who strive to fulfill it do not live in vain. A person who thinks, who knows, who understands, who dreams, who believes, looks around and wonders, even if he keeps it to himself, what kind of life would bring a man to hurt himself, his children, his peers—and not just from what we've observed during our brief service on earth, but also within the context of history, in a broader sense. Perhaps we might find a few scattered tribes of *uncivilized* people who, ignorant of everything, live like lesser animals, thus inevitably renouncing all of the highest, the most beautiful, the most luminous satisfactions, joys and achievements that can be provided by the perfectible human mentality, as opposed to the minds of beasts. And even observing ourselves, in our limited circles of relatives and acquaintances, we must admit that almost all of us live badly, without any comprehension of what our lives consist of spiritually and materially, without ever questioning why we do what we do, without ever analyzing

the goodness and the social utility of our work—which implies individual responsibility even if it is solely performed to meet the needs of living and feeding ourselves—without ever reflecting upon the almost sacred importance of each and every one of our acts, whether the more common acts of putting food into our mouths, quenching our thirst with healthy, pure water, or the poison of fermented drink—or more complex acts driven by our sensibility, which makes us instinctively seek out a union with another being, obeying the hidden natural laws that can complete or devastate entire existences, not just of individuals, but of families and generations. The few people who understand the intimate and mysterious meaning of life, or who at least interpret it in such a way as to illuminate the way for the less advanced, have the noble duty to not bury their conclusions on such a vital or quite simply relevant question regarding people and society, reached through study or meditation, within themselves. And the question of love, still enslaved by social laws and a person's thoughtlessness, is the fundamental question that especially concerns groups and individuals today.

[…] Many people, especially anarchists, have spoken of love and its necessary liberation—making an intelligent distinction between *free love* and *free unions*. Because this isn't about reforming, extending or modernizing a *law*, but rather, a new, broad anarchical concept that will be embraced and promoted for the happiness and health of the human race, for the full expansion of masculine or feminine vitality, for the realization of wider social victories that require the total liberty and full strength of individuals. In particular, it entails a more harmonious awareness and dignity among the far too many thoughtless beings that form the masses that, oppressed under the many yokes of today's society, dream and hope for a better future, full of peace, joy, and well-being, without doing anything about it, nor believing they are worthy enough to deserve it.

But our incessant discussions have almost always been founded on too narrow a base, built from personal points of view and trivial confessions of very personal events and experiences. Various controversies have concluded nothing and no light has been shed upon the intriguing discussion in such a way as to worthily highlight the disturbing attitude men have toward the problem of love—in its enslaved manifestations—or the reckless blindness of the community, which loves and continues the species with the same superficial indifference with which someone eats bits of hard-earned bread, or kills their brothers for causes they aren't even aware of.

Charles Albert, however, clearly understands the importance and breadth of the question that perhaps must be raised, addressed and settled before any libertarian or communist system could possibly be founded. He understands that "free love is not just a way to achieve sexual union free from the constraints of formalities or legal documents, or merely getting rid of these formalities." The composition of *free love* contains "something deeper, more complete, inasmuch as the freedom of love is not something so simple that it could be proclaimed in a paragraph of legal code."

Love, Albert concludes, "anticipates its liberation in the new society," because today, unfortunately, due to the miserable conditions of life faced by many beings who spend the years of their youth drained by the demands of unrewarding work, in humiliating misery, dependent upon a master, the joy of love is reduced to a transitory outpouring of the senses, to a tormented agitation never entirely satisfied, to the condemnation of mercenary or forced unions, which often leave an impure mark on a man's flesh for the rest of his life, and upon women, aside from the damage itself, a child without a father, or—something even worse—the secret curse of an infanticide.

Love—which is already in itself a form of subjugation, must be *not the purpose, but the joy of life* for individuals who are strong and aware. Albert shows how only total freedom from every sexual and economic constraint can restore love to being *love*, meaning total satisfaction of an individual desire, created from an instinctive harmony, heightened by the fusion of thoughts and bodies, and ennobled by the need for a loyal and friendly soul, which helps one through struggles and shares the joys that founding a new family brings to men and women.

Even today, amidst the hidden dangers and shames of bourgeois society, a *free* individual must understand how to enjoy his freedom to love, rebelling against the suffering generated by passion, stopping himself from going too far, enduring the struggles that love demands and poses. But someone who is still a slave, still dominated by economic and moral misery, must also be liberated economically in order to conquer the right to love and found a family without the infuriating concern of not being able to feed the children that will be born, of having to ask his partner to forgo her motherhood in order to earn her own bread. The enslaved man cannot even hope for love—which life is ready to give to all as it gives air—if he has not, at the least, first broken the most oppressive chains that keep him bound to the shackles the bourgeoisie has driven into every land to solidify the base of its already undermined institution.[22]

Married to Luigi Polli in 1902, Leda later spent twenty-three years in a relationship, both romantic and editorial, with Giuseppe Monanni, the father of her only child, Aini. Divorce and adultery were both illegal at the time, and as her association with Polli is generally considered to be an association based on protection and friendship rather than a sexual partnership, her concomitant union with Monanni does not seem all that peculiar. What is interesting about Leda's love life is the generally short-lived romantic adventures she had with several well-known intellectuals: a young socialist Benito Mussolini, the futurist painter Carlo Carrà, the rabbi and intellectual Emmanuel Taamrat, the Ethiopian interpreter Adem Surur, an Eritrean *askari* (soldier) who lived in Italy from 1927–1939, and probably a few others, as she lists two more names (Omar and Agaffari) in an unpublished and unfinished manuscript seemingly intended to tell more about the men she was involved with after she split from Monanni in 1926, aptly titled *A Woman and 4 Men from the East*.[23]

Leda's intimate companions were all intellectually or artistically cultivated men, and she began and left their love stories with no strings

---

22   Leda Rafanelli, preface to Charles Albert, *L'amore libero* (Milan: Casa Editrice Sociale, 1921), 6–12. Courtesy of the ABC.

23   Alessandra Pierotti, edt. Leda Rafanelli, *Tra letteratura e anarchia. Atti del convengo*, edt. Chessa Fiamma (Reggio Emilia: Biblioteca Panizzi, 2008), 37.

attached. Her flings with Carrà and Mussolini took place while she was still in a relationship with Monanni, and despite her frequent mentions of both her and him suffering from fits of jealousy, she quotes Monanni as steadfastly refusing to infringe upon her freedom to make choices regarding who to be with: "Do what you think is best for you. I don't ask you for promises, much less ask you to swear any vows."[24] In an autobiographical manuscript, she describes her relationship with Monanni as such:

> "[...]I think, between us, there is only a deep physical attraction, as well as a perfect union of Ideas. In terms of personality, desires, hopes, ways of understanding Life, we're very different. I am a faithful Muslim, He's an Atheist, and to Him, my Religion is "foolishness," as he says...During the holy, month-long fast of Ramadan, he has compassion for me, as if I was a mentally ill person...I will be fully in harmony with Life only when Destiny brings me back to Islam and has me marry someone within my religion. [...] It's true, we're not married. He would never really marry me according to these Laws that he doesn't recognize, nor could I marry Him under the Law of Islam. As a Muslim, I have no obligation of fidelity toward him."[25]

Just as Leda practiced Islam in accordance with her own personal interpretation, she also created and followed her own rules for sexual relationships. These rules, divulged from time to time through her work, did not seem to limit her so much as provide a framework within which she could confidently enter into a romantic affair. Love was not something sacred, so much as a pleasure in life: "Love is that which brings you joy, which doesn't make you suffer, which is necessary for life. Consider love like a cup of coffee: you drink it, it leaves a good taste in your mouth and makes your heart beat faster...but you don't love the empty cup. And love that can no longer give you anything is useless. Living off of memories and regrets is a way to hurt oneself. The Arab, instinctively, unconsciously, feels this way."[26]

---

24   Alberto Ciampi, edt., *Leda Rafanelli—Carlo Carrà, Un Romanzo: Arte e Politica in un Incontro Ormai Celebre*, 133.

25   Ibid., 126–127.

26   Leda Rafanelli (Djali), *L'amore in Oriente* (Unpublished manuscript, date unknown). Fondo "LR-M" conserved at the ABC.

Leda's interpretation of Arab femininity is evident in her personal collection of photographs. One could say Leda dressed modestly in the sense that she kept covered and didn't show off a lot of skin; yet the way she ornamented her body is blatantly exhibitionist. Whether draped in lengths of silk, wrapped in a full-length leopard print dress or sporting a heavily embroidered vest, her garments were not at all typical for a woman living in early twentieth-century Italy. But the fun doesn't stop there: she layered bracelets up to her elbows, matched by an equal number of beaded necklaces, and topped her bobbed hairdo with homemade headdresses: some featuring a scarab beetle in the middle, some with more demure geographic designs to complement the hooped earrings hanging from her ears. By no means self-conscious, Leda had her portrait taken a few times per year, and from the photographic evidence, her style seems to be influenced in equal parts by Scheherazade and Cleopatra. She poses in several with her arms behind her head; in others, she holds handfuls of jewelry or books, offering them towards the camera. In some shots, in which she must have invited the photographer over to her home, the central focus is the harem surrounding her, full of long tapestries covered with Arabic script and low furniture; other times the frame is simpler, and she merely tilts her head to one side, her hand on one hip or her body leaning against some sort of prop. Her postures are very feminine, yet certainly not reminiscent of anything in traditional Arab cultures. Instead, the photo collection that Leda built up over the decades provides a window into her female identity: exotic, flashy, and unlike anyone else in Italy at that time.

Along with her own image, Leda developed her own literary archetype of the "Eastern" woman: in harmony with nature, submissive, and dedicated to love. She spent more time creating her myth of the Arab woman as she gradually moved away from Italian anarchist circles, splintered and nearly washed away after two world wars and a few decades of fascism. With no passport and no savings, she was unable to leave Italy: therefore she created her own idealized land where human society mirrored the laws of nature (as she saw them) in her work, building and living a somewhat renegade female identity through Islam.[27] Despite her condemnation of colonialism, she advocated a romanticized conception of indigenous patriarchy, which she portrays as a simple, logical structure that provides clear roles for men and women.

---

27   Christiane Guidoni, "Leda Rafanelli: 'Donna e Femmina,'" 65.

Her characters repeatedly experience or recount how romance in European society is based on lies and illusions, while characters representing the "Eastern," chiefly Muslim, world experience a practical, if unimaginative, love founded upon fidelity and a firm division of roles. She idealized Arabs, depicting Muslim culture as better than European culture in every aspect of life, creating a world in which her own thoughts and feelings made sense.

***

> Unfortunately, I've never been beautiful. Perhaps if I had been an attractive woman like a thousand others, who knows what would have become of me, as a woman of love. Very small, with olive skin, brown eyes and hair, I've always been thin, deprived of elasticity: the only thing perfect about me, I would tell people, is my skeleton, with sharp, straight, lithe lines. If it had a few kilograms of flesh upon it, my skeleton could look something like a stylized Egyptian statuette.
>
> However, I had inside of me the instinctive art of "knowing how to please" males, the art that is practically a School for Muslim women. First and foremost there is the conviction, deeply rooted and sincere, of male superiority, the need to obey a Man, love him, serve him, almost lose oneself in him. The desire to give him joy, to laud his physical gifts, to appreciate the happiness that only a Lover can give. Furthermore, there is the idea to not ask for anything else but love, to not demand anything and to be happy to give, to always give without measuring. But only with a man from my same religion would I, one day, truly be what I was, naturally.[28]

***

In Leda's world, Muslim social order could be said to be based upon a "natural" difference between men and women and their respective roles. Oppression or disproportionate attribution of resources is not intrinsic to creating this division. As regards the gender divide in Islam, the Iranian

---

28   Leda Rafanelli, *Leda Rafanelli—Carlo Carrà, Un Romanzo: Arte e Politica in un Incontro Ormai Celebre*, 130–131.

scholar Mutahhari wrote: "Equality between men and women as regards their material and spiritual dignity is one thing, but parity, sameness, and uniformity of their rights is another. Over the course of history, 'equality' has taken on the meaning of 'sameness,' 'equivalence,' or 'uniformity.' Quality has been replaced by quantity. Attempts to grant women equal status under the criteria of 'masculinity' have led to the dissolution of her 'femininity.'"[29] This sounds very similar to Leda's argument of how bourgeois feminism sought to mold women in the image of men, in order to fulfill similar roles in a corrupt, patriarchal society.

Although it's not clear where she got her information from, Leda posits that, in "the East," it is the man who is exalted and objectified by the woman. She generally paints gender relations in the "East" as conducive to a simple definition of love, surrounded by little if any institutionalization. Especially given the use of adjectives such as "primitive" and "animalistic," Leda's representations of gender relations in her idealized culture are both ways to challenge how love and sexuality had been institutionalized in European cultures, as well as misinterpretations of inherently complex cultures. In the end, Leda never doubts a woman's power: "I believe that a woman can be the mistress of herself," she tells a friend in one of her autobiographical, unpublished manuscripts,[30] and she certainly did lead her own life in full control of her choices for nearly a century. Exactly what a woman's power was, however, and how nature intended for women to use it in this world, was a line of inquiry that zigzagged throughout Leda's work yet never led to any definitive conclusions.

***

"A forest catches fire from its own trees."
—Turkish proverb
Women, passing by, showing yourselves off as you walk in front of her—there's no use in wearing a mask. She understands all of you. She is also a woman—and also a female.

---

29   Murtada Mutahhari and Shahid Ayatu 'Llàh, *I diritti della donna nell'Islam*, trans. Abdu 'I-HadiPalazzi (Rome: Centro culturale islamico europeo, 1988), 26.

30   Leda Rafanelli, *La Grande Maestra* (unpublished manuscript, date unknown), 17. Conserved in a private collection owned and kindly made available by Fiamma Chessa.

And your sister in gender, in soul, in mind. She understands
every aspect of your complicated existence, all the traps of
fake simplicity and feigned indifference. She understands you,
all of you. She knows the truth you hide behind false words,
and she knows the meaning behind all of those words. You
can't fool her: she has uttered those same words herself.

She, if she wanted to, could reveal you fully—as you are,
without any veils—to your natural enemy; whether it's a man
or a male. But she will choose the most interesting among
the many, those females who have character, who represent
a type—whether through greatness or deprivation, virtue or
mediocrity; as there are also pure and strong women among
the masses of dead weight. And she will put them in their
place—on the altar or in martyrdom, in the store window or
in the saloon, in their true light, essentially. She knows how
to love and hate—she knows how to decide what she likes
and does not like in life, without pitying those who bruise her
exquisite sensibility too much. And she has so much pride in
herself that she would not consider it vain to humbly kneel
down in front of true women.

She is like life: she watches and observes, seemingly
indifferent, but forgets nothing. She mourns for failures in
her heart and does not waste her tears: her smile remains in
her soul to illuminate everything; yet contempt ripples her
fine lips and hatred flashes through her eyes, the color of ripe
dates. She is only jealous of that which she loves.

She is not a Christian, so she does not forgive. She is vin-
dictive, but she knows how to wait.

She was once young, she was once good, loved, and happy:
she was inspired by faith and ambition. But a woman's life is
short, and now she is tired. Now she sits in the sun, watching
the others pass by.

She is like a beggar: she does not ask for anything, but
waits, and accepts a few alms. She has lived her life lavishly,
and she is aware of this and still loves, even if she is miserly
with her joy today.

She sits down in the sun at the door of a temple and
watches, with a feline impassibility, like the Sphinx.

She no longer cares that time passes quickly. There is a bud growing near her. She is like a palm tree that has always lived alone in the ardent sand, and finally sees a soft tuft of leaves, green and tender just like her own, sprout up nearby. She is no longer alone in the desert: she will be part of an oasis.

When she is old, without any more of her sweet fruit—which she has always given as a gift to the many nomads in her life—she will bless the blossom of the new palm that will grow taller than her, as it already surpasses her in beauty and quality.

Meanwhile she enjoys the sun, the silence, the ardent solitude that the desert has stretched out around her.

Once she was named Djali, as then she fooled herself into thinking that she belonged to herself. Now she calls herself Sahara, the same name of the empire without subjects.

She has the sweet juice of the sacred palms in her fiber. And—like the rhapsodies of the oases—she loves to raise her voice amidst the surrounding silence.

This is why she tells stories.

She squints her eyes in the calm of the afternoon—already nearing evening—gathers her memories, puts them into words and expresses them as songs.

Today, a day of idleness and fasting, spent waiting for evening to arrive, in order to defeat time, which seems to pass very slowly as she longs for coffee, which she will take as soon as the moon appears—Djali—the woman who belongs to herself—Sahara—the woman who resembles the desert—sing the stories of other sisters, of other women, of other females—good and evil, happy and unhappy, victorious, victims and tyrants—much like herself. This sevenfold contrast, a prism of the soul, lies within every woman.

She has been happier than a queen, and now is unhappier than a beggar: she forms a complete parabola. She knows the whole arch. She knows that everything is useless and that what she says is also useless.

But it's so nice to speak to the desert!

Meanwhile, near her, other palms rise and seem to be listening. She speaks for them, but without a purpose, just...

to interrupt the silence, in order to distract herself from the buried ruins, on which her tough roots are anchored, to forget which cities, now buried, she has reigned over. It's so nice to speak to the desert, uselessly. Uselessly, as one lives, as one dies, as one loves, as one hates…all uselessly, as destiny wills it to be so.

First, she brought out the creatures of light and love—the creatures of abundance and pain, those that she has placed on the altar in her heart. She will rise to the vertex of her descent, and will come back down to earth—to the most unhappy, the saddest, the ugliest of all—to herself, a beggar of life, who has been happy, who was loved and who—even though she does not dare to hold out her hand—always expects something from life, for mercy's sake.

She has also become vile. She no longer has the superb strength of complete renunciation within her, although she has studied and understood the high philosophy of Gautama Buddha's words. The ancient energy has turned into sloth, the ancient independence has become slavery.

But this is what Destiny wills it to be. The forest shall catch fire from its own trees. And only cannibals and savages kill women that are no longer beautiful and young or, if they can still prove useful through working, sell them for a few spears. The civilized pretend to love them and value them.

—First day of Ramadan, 1339[31]

---

31   Leda Rafanelli, *Donne e Femmine*, 5–8.

CHAPTER V
The Intersection of Islam and Anarchism

As dawn broke, the crow of a mountain rooster awoke them, bringing them brusquely back to reality. At first they were surprised to find they weren't in their *angareb*, under the sloping roof of the *tukul*, but, instead, on the bare ground under a curtain of fronds. They felt that particular sense of loss and uncertainty that seizes the soul after a project is completed, after an unusual event happens, a feeling that sleep helps you to temporarily forget. Yet the joy of being free immediately came over both of them, and they remembered that they had escaped and looked at each other, laughing. They were free.

They performed their morning ablutions in a stream, reciting the first prayer of the day, and when they were ready to continue on with their journey, they realized they were hungry. There was nothing left of the food they had brought from home. They needed to buy something to eat, and Giohar asked Ibrahim for one of his *thalers*.

After two hours of walking, they met a woman on her way to sell her goods at the nearby *suk*. She sold them eggs and *kiccia* for a rather high price. They guessed they were near a Coptic village, a few kilometers from their own town. Luckily, the woman didn't ask them any questions, as she was happy enough to put the shining silver coin in her pocket in exchange for the food and a few smaller coins in change. She walked away quickly, pushing along the donkey laden with bags and baskets. The two boys exchanged glances, slightly worried, and then burst into laughter.

"It'd be funny if we accidentally ended up back home!" Giohar said.

"But you told me you knew these roads, and that you've already been to Asmara."

"I know the road that leads to Asmara as well as I know the road that leads to the Mosque!" Giohar responded, trying to make himself sound important. "But yesterday all I could think about was needing to escape, it didn't matter where, to get as far away as possible."

"But..." Ibrahim countered, bravely, "we're still just a few kilometers away from our village!"

"Look, you can see we're moving further away from the hills. We're up high now. Come on, we don't have any time to waste!"

They went down a narrow path that wound through the rugged, cultivated fields. Around noon, they arrived in a small village where—luckily for them—a wedding was being celebrated. They took advantage of the occasion to have a good lunch, as by tradition all who enter the banquet hall are treated as if they were invited guests. Nobody recognized them, and they were seated at a table on the groom's side, where they ate their fill and listened to the songs of praise improvised by a local poet. They rested for a few hours drinking *tegg* and tea. Giohar convinced Ibrahim that staying for dinner was the polite thing to do. After dinner, a large, ornately decorated metal tray was placed in the middle of the room, and all of the guests were invited to add their offering, as was customary. The two boys exchanged glances. They had no option but to do their duty.

Without anyone noticing, Ibrahim unwrapped a *thaler* from the knot of his *barracano* and placed it on top of the others. But as soon as he returned to his seat, Giohar whispered in his ear: "Give me a *thaler*, Ibrahim, because I have to do my part, too."

And Ibrahim took the third *thaler* out of his *barracano*.

They day after the party, they continued on their way with one *thaler* and a little bit of change left in their pockets. But they didn't feel anxious about it.

The laws of hospitality that governed the villages scattered across the Eritrean highlands ensured that whenever the two boys presented themselves on the threshold of a *tukul* to wish the family good morning or good evening, they would be invited to enter and sit at the table if the family was in the middle of a meal. Ibrahim hesitated, but Giohar didn't need any encouragement. He always told a different story about what village they were from, while Ibrahim stayed silent, afraid he might contradict his friend.

"But why do you lie so much?" he asked as they left a hut where they had just been served a snack.

"Should I tell them we're going to Asmara? Our families have probably already sent someone out to look for us, and we have to make sure these people don't get suspicious and start talking about us. So from now on, let's just say we're two Coptic students. If we get rid of these turbans and hide our *subah* (the Mohammedan rosary), we can sing for these people and tell them we're on an educational trip, we'll make lots of money in alms." Ibrahim was convinced Giohar's idea was a good one. All Ibrahim wanted was to go to Massawa, get on a steamer and sail off to unknown lands and undiscovered beaches. He only thought of the home he had left and his mother at nighttime, as he laid in a strange *tukul* or under the light of the moon, trying unsuccessfully to fall asleep.

One evening, they hadn't found any huts along their path, and as the sun set they entered an old, abandoned Mosque. They felt intimidated and embarrassed in the vast, empty room. Their footsteps didn't even make a sound as their bare feet crossed the dusty and bumpy floor: everything inside was quiet and desolate. They two boys didn't dare speak and rouse the echo of life. They had always seen the Mosque full of crowds of the faithful, vibrating with the voices and songs of the wise men who read the Qur'an. Finding themselves all alone in that sacred enclosure as night fell gave them a vague sense of fear and despair.

Of course, Gihoar didn't want his traveling companion to see how afraid he was inside. Ibrahim, too, wanted to show

Giohar how brave he was. Seemingly calm, they exchanged a
few words, whispering:

"I think it's time we should sleep."

"Right. Let's go to sleep."

They laid down in a corner on top of some old mats (forgotten remnants of former splendor), watching the hesitant
light of dusk grow dimmer through the broken, dusty glass
window panes. But when even that faint light had gone out
and night had wrapped itself around every image and every
silhouette, the two boys felt something in their hearts that
seemed, strangely enough, like regret for having run away
from their safe and familiar homes.

Their minds filled with memories of a thousand scary
stories they used to tell while lying awake at night, although
neither dared to talk about them aloud. People said that
whenever the faithful abandoned a Mosque, the Devil would
come along and take it over. But when a jackal's howl reached
their ears, the two boys could no longer contain their fear.
They jumped up, stretching out into the darkness to find each
other—pretending, of course, that they had just woken up—
and felt great relief to hear the sound of their own voices.

"A jackal!" Ibrahim said. "He's really howling!"

"Let him yelp!" Giohar said, feigning indifference. "The
door is closed, for better or worse, and it can't get in. A jackal
can't pass through walls like the Devil can."

"Be quiet!" Ibrahim yelled, trembling.

"Right before I fell asleep," Giohar continued, "I felt
someone pulling on my coat. Then I felt a hand slowly pass
across my face…"

"Shut up!" Ibrahim repeated, now in a cold sweat.

"…but I wasn't afraid! It's no secret that the Devil visits
abandoned Mosques during the night."

They couldn't fall back asleep, or even pretend to. They
needed to feel the other's presence, they needed to talk so
they wouldn't think and think. The two poor boys ended up
hugging, like two brothers. Only when the sun broke through
the sky did they stretch out comfortably on the mound of old
mats, cover their heads with the darkness of their coats, and

fall into a sleep so deep that even if the Devil himself walked into the Mosque and shook them with all of his frightening might, they wouldn't have woken up.[1]

***

To See the World (*Vedere il Mondo*) has few, if any, political undertones. In fact, it was published in 1951 as an illustrated children's book by Antonio Vallardi Editore, a commercial publishing house. Yet this and other stories Leda wrote for young readers provide a major, although indirect, source of information regarding her interpretation of Islam, of how she imagined people thought and acted in Muslim societies, and how she considered their rules and customs to be superior to those followed in European societies. Indeed, Giohar and Ibrahim are two Eritrean Muslim boys, yet they interact with members of several other faiths throughout the book, painting a picture of intercultural dialogue and harmonious interfaith relations, elements that were not widely valued in Europe.

Leda had never travelled to the Horn of Africa, yet Italy's straggling attempts at colonizing foreign territory had widened channels of communication and exchange between East Africa and the peninsula in the early twentieth century. The "failed" Italo-Ethiopian war of 1895–1896 was compensated for in 1912, when what remained of the Ottoman Empire ceded the provinces of Tripolitania, Fezzan, and Cyrenaica to Italy. Italy would later christen this area as Libya, a term the ancient Greeks used to refer to North Africa. Thus Leda's choice to situate fictional adventures in East and Northern Africa reflected an attempt to counter imperialistic justifications that the "savage" civilizations living in these lands were in dire need of European management.

Young Giohar, feeling unloved by his stepmother and father, decides to run away from home. He convinces his friend Ibrahim, the Gallant to his Goofus, to come along by promising him that they're going to make it to the port city of Massawa, get on a ship and finally see the world. Ibrahim accordingly raids the family coffers and the two go vagabonding around the local region, getting lost and running into lions. They

---

1   Leda Rafanelli, *Vedere il mondo* (Milan: A. Vallardi, 1951), 21–26. Fondo "LR-M" conserved at the ABC.

eventually wind up in their home town, only to set off again in a different direction and have another round of wacky adventures.

In this relatively sedate narrative, at least as compared to her political work, Leda gradually introduces words and concepts from the cultures of Eritrea, writing the terms phonetically in Italian without offering a glossary at the end: she draws the young reader into an intercultural context, in which it's okay to not understand every reference that comes one's way. The details describing everyday practices in Muslim culture likely came from a combination of her exchanges with friends from Eritrea and Ethiopia, what she had picked up from reading, or perhaps her own experiences in Egypt. With a mission of cultural diplomacy overshadowing concerns for accuracy, she exposes her audience to another way of life while subverting the predominant colonial narrative.

To See the World is just one of many works written for young audiences set somewhere in the upper half of Africa that Leda wrote and published, or just wrote, beginning in the late 1920s. The short story *Ain-Nar*—which she translates into Italian as *occhi di fuoco* (eyes of fire)—focuses on a blind young man who sits on the side of the road, cursing a certain "Fatima" all day long. The narrator, intrigued, asks a few Italian expatriates living in Massawa what they know about this Ain-Nar character, and is told that the young man's blindness is the result of a tragic incident involving passionate love and jealous rages. Yet, two years later, when the narrator directly asks Ain-Nar (whose real name is Abdallah) what happened, he learns that the injury was just an accident caused by a young girl named Fatima, during a friend's wedding celebration, thus dispelling the dramatic myths created by cultural outsiders.

In *Abu Nuas Is Unlucky* (*Abu Nuas non ha fortuna*), the greed of a relatively well-off man named Abu Nuas is inspired when he sees a beggar making a nice fortune off of two *zubbàt* sitting in a cafe, who were touched by the beggar's display of religious piety. Abu Nuas decides to follow the *zubbàt* around and wait for the right moment to show them that he, too, is pious, in hopes of receiving a gold coin. Yet the opportunity never arises, and instead, Abu Nuas accidentally blesses the two government officials with a recitation usually reserved for funeral rites, irritating them and making himself look like a fool: "'I have no luck!' he said to himself, lifting his eyes to the sky. And he saw thousands upon thousands of stars shining like the gold coins he would never have."[2]

---

2   Leda Rafanelli, *Abu Nuas non ha fortuna* (unpublished manuscript, date

About fifty of Leda's fictional slices of life in North and East Africa were published, under the pen name Zagara Sicula, between 1930–1940 in the *Children's Courier (Corriere dei piccoli)*, a weekly children's magazine based in Milan that paid its contributors. Each only one to two thousand words long, these stories take on a moralistic, didactic tone commonly used when addressing young audiences: yet in these pieces, it is the indigenous protagonists who provide the morals, serving as teachers, or examples, or even counter-examples for young readers. Leda also created fiction featuring characters from Muslim cultures for adult audiences such as the novel *The Oasis* and short stories such as "The Rhabdomancer," which will be discussed at length in Chapter 7.

Through the Muslim characters Leda presents in her work, we can see three elements that are particularly evident in her interpretation of Islam: the inherent dignity of human beings; the claim that the "natural" social order of Islamic societies was superior to the order established through European social institutions; and a ubiquitous, yet not exactly pessimistic, sense of fatalism. Her characters constantly evoke Allah's will, the idea that *what will happen will happen*—an idea that presents an interesting juxtaposition to the anarchist vocation, particularly as a propagandist, to be proactive in fostering large-scale revolutionary change. Yet perhaps this is less a juxtaposition than psychological relief, a way to remain patient in the face of continued oppression from society and government.

Leda's interest in Muslim cultures was not just confined to the literary domain, nor was it merely a reaction against the arrogance of colonialism. Although not an outwardly utopian anarchist, Leda embraced the Islamic faith as if embracing her true heritage, or even an alternative version of what the modern world could be. Through personalizing the faith and romanticizing Muslim cultures she created her own idea of what it meant to live according to the principles of Islam, and dutifully set out to express that identity in her daily life. Given the fact that there was no Muslim community in Italy during the early twentieth century, nobody challenged her interpretation or right to create her spiritual practice as she saw fit, although her fellow anarchists did not necessarily understand her need for religious affiliation.

The photographic record and her autobiographical writings shows that she fully expressed her self-selected Muslim identity through her dress and daily habits until the end of her life: in a 1967 letter, for example, she

unknown). Fondo "LR-M" conserved at the ABC.

describes her latest health problems to a friend, complaining about how the doctor urged her to eat meat despite the fact that she was faithfully observing the Ramadan fast.[3] Leda, however, did not publish propaganda to promote Islam or justify her spiritual convictions. Flashy clothes aside, Islam was an inner journey for her, a space of spirituality that existed beyond the public political sphere, the *femmina* spirituality to her *donna* politics, where she was able to keep her religious convictions pure, meaning uncontaminated by institutional authority and unconstrained by infringements upon her personal freedom. Much of her writing on the subject, aside from the children's stories and the aforementioned publications, remained unpublished, including several unedited book manuscripts, poems, essays, and reaction pieces concerning current events in Muslim countries.

The development of her Muslim identity, just like the development of her anarchist identity, depended heavily on her reading material. Her personal library contains a heavily annotated copy of *Arabic Spoken in Egypt,* printed in 1913 by a Milanese publisher, full of dried four leaf clovers as well as little slips of paper with language exercises on them. In these exercises, the Arabic is written in the right-hand column as the Italian translation on the left dictates: *There are four sciences: Knowledge of divine law, for religions; Medicine, for bodies; Stars, for the ages; Grammar, for language.* The next exercise reads: *Good writing is a source of wealth for the poor, an ornament for the rich, and perfection for the great.*

Aside from a dozen Arabic dictionaries and other language learning materials, the Qur'an was indeed an important part of her personal library. In her 1915 pamphlet *Down with the War* (*Abbasso la guerra*), Leda writes: "Talmud...Torah...Qur'an—books that are, more than religious texts, Civil Codes, as guides for many Eastern peoples."[4] The Christian bible is, of course, markedly absent from this list, and its exclusion does not mark a fallacy of categorical logic so much as an intentional snub, given the Catholic Church's effusive and downright political presence in Italian society. Leda may very well have sought moral guidance from the Qur'an to enrich her anarchical existence, particularly through the difficult burdens of two world wars, decades of fascism, and family tragedies.

---

3   Alberto Ciampi edt., *Leda Rafanelli—Carlo Carrà, Un Romanzo: Arte e Politica in un Incontro Ormai Celebre*, 13.
4   Leda Rafanelli, *Abbasso La Guerra* (pamphlet) (Milan: Societa Editrice Milanese, 1915). Fondo "LR-M" conserved at the ABC.

Without external pressure to categorize, define, or defend her faith, Leda was able to use it and adapt it as she pleased, drawing support and inspiration from its teachings and modifying it to fit her needs. She did not join a mosque or faith community, nor did she seek a guru who would help her to elaborate or interpret her understanding of Islam. There is, sociologically speaking, a big difference between being a member of a faith and being a member of a faith community. To our knowledge, she didn't develop any close relationships with fellow Muslims until the 1930s, when she began a romantic relationship with Adem Surur.

Anarchists are well-known critics of religion, and Leda was no exception to this rule. She expressly identified herself as "anticlerical," and some of her strongest work focuses on the corruption of the Catholic Church. For example, in the pamphlet *Clerical Chastity (Castità Clericale)*, she describes how priests abuse young men and women. A proposed reform that would allow male clerics to marry and have wives was never going to pass, she posits, as it would cost the ecclesiastic class their special place in society and transform them into ordinary working stiffs, which would ultimately work against the image of dogmatic authority:

> As free spirits, we will always object to how religious movements—which over the years have moved away from their legendary and luminous origins, degraded and darkened by their own clergy—disguise entirely material interests with statements that are more useful to certain men, certainly, than the Gods they claim to represent.
>
> Priests do not neglect their ordinary human needs—they have no faith, only religion. Catholicism is a great power and its phalanxes of men and women who are tonsured, cloistered, and regimented into numerous orders, constitute a huge force that could overwhelm all other religious and social energies.
>
> People who study these problems begin by saying that "appearances are deceiving" and that the Catholic church, considered a "giant" among other religious faiths, is in fact weak and deficient like giant humans, heavy with its physical bulk and dim-witted...In fact, religious advocates, whose power is strengthened by the laws of every government, do not tolerate opposition, do not respond to harsh criticism, and while they know well how to affirm ideas to their advantage,

they defend themselves by invoking religious dogma and the indisputable will of the papacy, and certainly don't make their believers aware of the political origins of their version of the truth, which has nothing to do with Real History.[5]

Leda's criticism of religion is clearly a criticism of its implementation by those with agendas outside of the spiritual realm, rather than the principles or stories presented in the texts upon which the religion was based. Transferring this line of critique to members of her own faith, Leda also wrote essays criticizing imams and authorities in the Muslim world, as in a 1957 piece discussing the Ismaili Muslims and the transfer of power from Aga Khan III to Aga Khan IV: "Who is your God? Who is your Prophet? Who is your Imam? Only true Muslims would know how to respond to these and other questions. But when asked who is your Imam, how do the Ismaili worshippers respond? Certainly not with the formula established by our Law: El Qur'an Imami. Instead they would respond: Our Imam is a man, with our weaknesses, our shortcomings, our vices, multiplied by one hundred due to his incredible wealth that we, as poor deluded people, have procured for him, so that he may vegetate in sloth, enjoy an entirely materialistic life, infest the world with many useless parasites while remaining insensitive to human struggle, misery, and aspirations."[6]

There still remains, however, the fundamental contradiction created by the fact that Leda was a practicing Muslim: furthermore, we cannot consider her merely anticlerical for she explicitly, repeatedly, extends her critique of religion to *all* religions: "All religions are absurd legends, decorated with strange poetry, based on nonexistent creatures and endowed with all sorts of supernatural, mysterious, and therefore non-negotiable powers and virtues. An individual who has a healthy and active intellect does not need to work too hard to understand that a deep pit of lies yawns underneath the mystic veils."[7]

Leda was also aware of this discrepancy, and alluded to it a few times in her writing. In one such case, she wrote a letter to the editor of the

5   Leda Rafanelli, *Castità Clericale* [pamphlet], 1910. Fondo "LR-M" conserved at the ABC.

6   Leda Rafanelli, *Idolatria Assurda,* (unpublished manuscript, circa 1957). Fondo "LR-M" conserved at the ABC.

7   Leda Rafanelli, "Contro il dogma" in *Per l'idea nostra: Raccolta di articoli e bozzetti di propaganda* (Florence: Libreria Rafanelli-Polli E C., 1905), 23–24. Fondo "LR-M" conserved at the ABC.

Corriere della Sera in 1963, right after the newspaper printed an article describing Leda as extravagant and, what's worse, did so using the past tense. An eighty-two year old Leda set the record straight as such: "My name is, *not my name 'was'*, Leda Rafanelli, as I am still alive and, *inshallah,* in excellent health, thanks to my lifestyle: nourishing my body with the yoga method and practicing the ritual of *ramadan.* I was not *'a fanatic* of the Muslim religion' because I *am* a faithful and practicing follower of Islamic law, expert in the Arabic language, and still an individualist anarchist activist. Perhaps my 'extravagance' is due to the fact that I have remained deeply faithful to my ideas and to my Mohammedan religion."[8] As Leda had no interest in following dogma of any kind, it makes sense that she would swim against the current of her own anti-institutionalism, brushing it all off as a mere "extravagance."

Nevertheless, the five pillars of Islam do not contradict the basic principles of anarchism: in order to be considered a true Muslim, a person must declare that Allah is the only god and Muhammad is Allah's messenger; strive to pray 5 times a day; fast for Ramadan; make it to Mecca if circumstances permit; and give alms (*zakat*) as part of a greater goal to eliminate inequality. These pillars are commonly referred to as ways of teaching piety, self-restraint, and humility, not to mention the importance of mutual assistance. If freely accepted by the practitioner, none of these principles present an overt conflict of interest with anarchism, aside from the sticky question of god.

Historically and geographically speaking, Islam and anarchism haven't had a lot of time to commingle. Anarchism itself is a rather new and malleable movement that made its official debut on the European stage less than two centuries ago. Islam, on the other hand, has been around for over 1400 years, and despite eight centuries of influence in Mediterranean regions, had retreated to North Africa and the Middle East by the 1700s.

Some scholars count a total of nine separate sects of Islam that arose after the death of Muhammad, divisions that gradually boiled down to the Sunni/Shi'ite categories used today. Throughout history, regional interpretations of the religion have placed different degrees of emphasis on tribal origin, blood ties, and Arab nationalism, among other factors specific to a local context. And, just as Christianity mixed with indigenous

---

8   Leda Rafanelli, letter to the editor in the *Corriere della Sera*, April 30 1963 edition, page 5. Fondo "LR-MM-MLF" conserved at the ABC.

spiritualities after evangelization in Latin American and Africa, the historical legacies of pre-Islamic cultures also had a major influence on how Islam was implemented, as evidenced by how Zoroastrian elements intermingle with Islam in Iran, for example. The range of interpretations of Islam could be seen as part of a continuum, with extremism and puritanism on one end, moderatism in the center, and a variety of other hybrid or even nonreligious interpretations on the other end. One suggestion for drawing the line between moderate and puritan interpretations is to assess whether or not women are respected as "dignified and autonomous beings" under that specific interpretation.[9]

If the basic principles of Islam and anarchism—the five pillars and the general concept of anti-authoritarian autonomy (whether cooperative or individualistic), respectively—are not mutually exclusive, one wonders whether their convergence would reveal a few overlapping areas, perhaps ways that these ideologies could be used to support and strengthen one another. The idea of a higher power, of course, needs to be addressed first: how can someone worship a god, in this case Allah, while claiming to be anti-authoritarian? How does devotion to God fit in with the abolition of hierarchy?

What is first and foremost important to an anarchist reading of Islam, with all due respect to the range of its adaptations, is a deconstruction of the concept of spiritual authority. The energy with which one shouts the slogan "No gods, no masters" is likely to be inspired by acts of oppression or exploitation committed by human beings in the earthly realm. Frustration with "God" or "gods" is more appropriately attributed to human beings who claim to represent divine powers and, accordingly, use their power to abuse other human beings. Throughout the history of every religion, corrupt, nasty, and violent human beings have committed atrocities under the banners of religious right: yet who can definitively say what the holy spirit had to do with these atrocities.

Indeed, one could argue that, in the Qur'an, Allah prohibits subservience to another human being. Lacking an "official" English translation of the Qur'an, and with full acknowledgment of my own ignorance concerning its allusions and context, the most we can do in this chapter is point out paths for further inquiry. In that spirit, Arberry's translation of the Qur'an provides the following for Surah 23:35: "If you obey a

9   Khadel Abou El Fadl, *The Great Theft: Wrestling Islam from the Extremists* (New York: Harper Collins, 2007), 274.

mortal like yourselves, then you will be losers. What, does he promise you that when you are dead, and become dust and bones, you shall be brought forth? Away, away with what you are promised! There is nothing but our present life; we die, and we live, and we shall not be raised up."[10] Is such discouragement of obeying a "mortal like yourselves" an indication that humans are not meant to submit to the authority of other human beings?

In the Qur'an, there is an evident hierarchy established of divine over mortal, as stated in Surah 30:35: "God is He that created you, then He provided for you, then He shall make you dead, then He shall give you life; is there any of your associates does aught of that? Glory be to Him! High be He exalted above that they associate!"[11] From a preliminary review, the idea of establishing a direct relationship to god, without the intercession of clerical interpreters, seems to be pervasive throughout the Qur'an, not unlike protestant versions of Christianity. If the Arabic word "Islam" does indeed translate to "submission to God," then the potential roles and applications of human authority, thus submission to other humans, are limited, if not prohibited.

When mentioned in academic works, Leda is often referred to as a Sufi, though she only self-identifies as Muslim or "Mohammedan" whenever she brings up the subject in her own words.[12] The Sufi label is not entirely misplaced, however, as Sufism has historically been more attuned to the inner, spiritual sphere of Islam: "[Sufism] is above all else an Islamic method of internal perfection, of balance, a source of deeply felt and gradually ascending fervor. Far from being an innovation or divergent, parallel path to canonical practice, it is primarily a resolute mark of a category of stricken souls, thirsty for God, moved by the shock of his grace to live only with him and thanks to him within the framework of his connected, internalized, tested law."[13]

Leda created her own Islam using influences from a variety of different contexts: "I know well that, inside of me, lives my soul, from many centuries ago that have since crumbled to dust, I know well that I love

10   A. J. Arberry, *The Koran Interpreted: A Translation*, 1955, xhtml markup by Arthur Wendover on May 1, 2003. http://web.archive.org/web/20071219022352/ http://arthursclassicnovels.com/arthurs/koran/koran-arberry10.html.

11   Ibid.

12   Gabriele Mandel Khan, *Leda Rafanelli. Tra letteratura e anarchia. Atti del convengo,* edt. Chessa Fiamma (Reggio Emilia: Biblioteca Panizzi, 2008), 143.

13   Ibid., 144.

only what I've loved in my distant Past: 'my' Pyramids, 'my' Ruins of Karnak, 'my' Sphinx, for me, they are the most powerful and most harmonious expression of Art that has glorified Humans, making them— only because of Art—superior to the other Animals created, intelligent, instinctive, but which have not received the gift, from Allah, of the Light, the Flame, the Strength, the Beauty that Humans have because of Art."[14] At heart, she wasn't concerned about what specific label to put on her spirituality, nor whether or not ancient Egyptian influences could be considered valid elements of Islam. If religion is a human creation, why shouldn't humans have the power to continue shaping it, creatively constructing it as they deem appropriate?

Without prejudice to its anti-institutionalism, anarchism is conducive to multiple identities. Malatesta was just one of the many proponents of anarchism without adjectives, implying a flexibility of interpretation and ideological collaboration, whether communist, collectivist, mutualist, syndicalist, pacifist, or even, perhaps, spiritual.

Likewise, despite the fact that extremism is all too frequently, and all too erroneously, used as a synonym for Islam, anti-authoritarian interpretations of Islam should produce no more surprise than parallel interpretations of Christianity. A supra-human power is an entirely different concept than authority imposed by one human being over another, generally for manipulative and/or exploitative purposes. Despite the institutional ambitions of many world religions, spiritual concerns belong to a parallel dimension that does not negate the principles of anarchism.

***

They came to a village that was, unfortunately, where the sheik, who had hosted them before, lived. Both Giohar and Ibrahim would rather have walked twice as long than pass through that village. But it was located right along their way, and the gendarmes had no reason to avoid it. The two prisoners thus had to undergo the shame of being caught in the severe—and yet indulgent—gaze of the sheik, who came towards the group of curious onlookers, and after interrogating the two guards, addressed them with kind words.

---

14   Alberto Ciampi, *Leda Rafanelli—Carlo Carrà, Un Romanzo: Arte e Politica in un Incontro Ormai Celebre*, 119.

"And now that you have tried to leave your homes without the permission of your parents, go back to your families without any bad intentions and think about how, once you're men, you'll be able to travel. See the world with the experience and strength needed for that sort of venture. I had suspected that you were lying to me when I first met you, but I let myself be fooled by how honest you sounded," and he turned to Giohar, "while you were talking to me. Your lie is the worst page of your story, and it is worse than the theft that you," and he turned to Ibrahim, "committed against your own family. The end of your adventure shall guide you in the future."

Seeing that both of their faces were red and bruised, he asked the smiling *zaptie* what had happened, who responded in short:

"We gave them the rifles to carry, and they started rough-housing like roosters. If I hadn't broken it up, they'd have blown out their own brains!"

"That's terrible!" the sheik said, in a very serious tone of voice. "As peers, despite the fraternity that your common fate should have inspired, you fight like enemies? You need discipline. Chances are I may go myself to speak with your fathers. Where are you from?"

The two gendarmes answered for them. They told him the name of the town the boys had escaped from. "Yes, I'll go there…soon. And if you see their parents tell them, on my behalf, that they shouldn't be beaten. They're just boys. Beating them would only make them worse. It's better to be indulgent and keep a closer eye on them in the future. Understood?" He then turned back to the two guilty boys.

"Yes, wise sheik, we understand. Please come to our village soon!" Ibrahim said, moved, kissing the old man's hand.

"Yes, come soon!" Giohar added. Even the condescending *curbasc* moved closer to him, feeling the need for some support and moral protection. "I'll tell my father about you, please come!"

And now it was time to start walking again. But just then, the sheik's good wife—as wise as her husband—came forward with a basket full of food. The boys were so hungry that they wanted to pounce upon it immediately. Observing the imploring glances of his wife, the sheik graciously decided to invite the entire party to dinner, and once again, together with the two *zaptie*, Giohar and Ibrahim passed the best hours of their adventure in that hospitable home.[15]

***

Leda's use of Islam, particularly as a literary theme, bears traces of idealization and glorification. From the wise sheik to the benevolent gendarmes—certainly not how gendarmes would be portrayed in propaganda set in Italy—she unfurls a romantic vision of social dynamics in the Muslim world. Yet her romanticism was rooted in her reality, for she had made Islam a part of her inner world, where compassion, solidarity, and the struggle for justice reigned supreme. This was the religion of Leda Rafanelli, and it required no justification or approval from other anarchists or Muslims.

---

15   Leda Rafanelli, *Vedere il mondo* (Milan: A. Vallardi, 1951), 76–78. Fondo "LR-M" conserved at the ABC.

CHAPTER VI
Individualism and Futurism: Compagni in Milan

We had gotten into the habit of meeting at Caffè del Centro
at the end of the day. That Caffè was located on the corner of
Via Carlo Alberto and some other street. During the evenings,
it attracted a rather strange, heterogeneous clientele which
took up numerous tables in the back of the large Room, practically a reserved area. With a cup of Coffee (which in those
days cost three cents), we took over our spot for the entire
evening, and for the entire evening the discussions and debates took on such a high tone (in terms of volume) that the
waiter assigned to that area (a serious and refined young man
who earned very little in tips) looked for any opportunity to
stop and listen, since this regular crowd was so different from
those who sat in the central Room and at the Bar: married
couples passing through, business men who drank their Coffee standing up at the counter and then left. With only our
crowd, the place wouldn't have made much money!

Every table had its own personality and was guarded by
those who sat around it, almost as if they were divided into
categories, but all *bohemians*. Carlo reigned over the table
of the Artists. He was a Painter, but sympathized with us,
the Anarchists. And, when he caught a few phrases amidst
the clamor of voices, he would hurl a "That's not true!" our
way, which, in the end, amused us. He smiled even when he

seemed irritated, and his smile was fresh, youthful, just like his ironic and intelligent expression. He looked like a large sleeping cat, sitting on the red velvet sofa all wrapped up in his brown robe. As it was Winter, He—like me—suffered from the cold, and he kept his arms folded inside of his sleeves, like a monk. He observed everyone, he contradicted everyone, but especially one elegant and polite young man—a Poet, who had taken a spot at the *intellectual* table. His name was Fausto, he wasn't yet twenty years old, and they called him the "Poetino." He had a naïve goodness to him and was nice to everyone, engaging in erudite and brilliant conversation. His verses had already been published in literary journals and Magazines. He was enthusiastically working on a volume of poetry. He would say that Poetry was the purest joy in Life, "the passion of the Soul above and beyond the pettiness of daily life." But after each one of his sublime statements the Painter would jump in, booming out a "That's not true!" Fausto, however, paid no mind to those irreverent interruptions, and continued to recite quotations and verses of Leopardi and Gozzano, in the silence that had suddenly descended. Even the Waiter, and a few other customers, would come closer to listen: and the Painter, shaking his head, both empathetic and patronizing, would murmur: "Ah, come on, you pathetic romantic!"

During calmer evenings, the Poetino would also recite his own verses, and we would listen, indulgent and conflicted, as most of us listeners were of *extreme* Ideologies. Fausto had a super-human concept of Love: "Artistic inspiration is person-ified by a beautiful, pure Maiden, who illuminates the Poet's Life with her Love, and guides him towards Timeless Poet-ry." The Painter would look at him ironically and smile, and indeed, not many people agreed with the Poetino.

A few other Men presided over the Intellectual's table. No longer young, they were authoritative in their judgments, and attractive through their way of expressing themselves, confident and, I would say, unquestioning. At heart They represented Criticism: you could say they criticized everything and everyone. They were always nice to us, always *against the current* when it came to Art, much how we Libertarians were when it came to Life. One of these Individuals, who would say next to nothing all evening long as he drank his coffee drop by drop, had a sad and distracted air about him: he committed suicide a little while later, shooting himself with a pistol. For as much as that event saddened us, I can no longer remember his name.

Near our table, close to the presumptuous red sofa of the Artists, there was another little table in the corner, flanking the arcade that led to the central lounge. Every evening a few Fellows—sometimes old, sometimes young—came to sit at this table. They were almost never the same two people: they didn't say anything, they didn't start anything with anyone, they just listened, and left a little bit before we Libertarians left. They were policemen who came to monitor only the Anarchists, surely without understanding what we said, as we talked about a little bit of everything but never made our own problems public. But they were protecting Society as they listened and, in any case, had very little to report back to their *superiors.*

I was the only Woman who attended those gatherings that, in the end, didn't really mean much to us. Together with my Compagno at the time, a very young man who had come to Milan with me, I directed an anarchist periodical that the Police had already sequestered twice, and this is why we were under *surveillance.* Our Compagni, well known figures in the Movement, would come and go every evening. Often the Workers from the Print shop where we printed our Newspaper would also stop by.

The most interesting personality there was undoubtedly my Friend—which only our close friends knew was my partner. He was barely twenty years old, handsome, serious, and sparse with his words. Sitting next to me, he would spend hours reading and correcting drafts of the newspaper. He felt a certain fondness for the Painter, whose character and temperament were so different from his own, and would respond to his blustering criticism with an enigmatic smile, without ever getting involved in the general discussions. And the Painter also acted disdainful toward Him, but in such a way that he almost seemed to be sympathizing with our Ideas.

"Don't you have anything to say? You're quite stingy with your words, you can't give us more than one of your Mona Lisa smiles?" Perhaps he sensed that there was a more intimate and loving connection between us, but he wasn't sure of it. He watched us, however, with his penetrating, ironic, almost mocking gaze. By chance he found out that I was a few years older than my Friend and, one evening, on the sofa, he leaned toward me and whispered: "Do you enjoy taking Adolescents as lovers?" I looked at him, surprised, yet not irritated by his brazenness.

With his long beard, the large woolen scarf around his neck, the frayed tobacco-colored robe, his small hands poking out of the wide monkish sleeves—which he used as a muff while walking down the street—he looked like an old man, despite his fresh, sensual mouth, which betrayed his youth.

"Well, you certainly are no longer an adolescent, and haven't been one for a long time, either." I responded, to hurt Him. But he laughed.

"No," he responded in a low voice. "I'm a Man."

The chattering Compagni around us covered the sound of our words. And the Painter continued:

"I've been watching you two…You're very different. He's simple, skeptical, and earnest. You're strange and complicated. Even your way of dressing. But I like you this way."

I've always liked dressing *unfashionably*. I usually wore comfortable black clothes, with several exotic necklaces coiled around my neck. I would put on large gold hoop earrings and wear Egyptian coins on my cuffs. Almost everyone, however, was unaware that I belonged to Islam, by custom, ancestry, and Religion. The Painter continued, under his breath: "Really, you intrigue me…I'd like to paint your portrait. Do you want to come to my Studio tomorrow?"

"No," I replied flatly. I sensed that my Compagno was not as distracted as he seemed to be and, without showing it, was listening.

Without another word, the Painter drifted away, returning to the others in his *department*.

"What was that about?" Guido asked me. Guido was one of my dearest Compagni and had observed, without understanding, that the Painter had suggested something to me, and that I had responded in the negative.

"Nothing," I replied, and smiled at him, since Guido, though He was very young, was quite intuitive.[1]

***

Thus Leda remembers her first encounters with Carlo Carrà (1881–1966), with whom she had a short relationship in 1912, in the political and cultural hotbed of Milan in 1910. Several decades into the now booming industrial revolution, Italy was in the midst of the Giolittian era, named for the relatively progressive Giovanni Giolitti (1842–1928) who served three terms as prime minister between 1903 and 1914. Unlike many of his predecessors, Giolitti refrained from outwardly oppressing syndicalism and socialism, instead employing a tactic called *transformismo* (transformism) to bring together disparate factions of the left and right. He went as far as to court various socialist leaders to serve in his cabinet, although when asked, Turati declined, wary of the implications of working within a bourgeois state structure.

While focusing largely on the development of the national economy, Giolitti also promoted the 1912 electoral reform bill, which introduced something similar to universal male suffrage. Giolitti's popularity, however, had already started to subside due to the high, bloody costs entailed in wresting Libya from Turkish control, a war that demanded more, financially and in terms of human life, and lasted longer than originally expected. Since its launch in 1911, the Libyan campaign had, in fact, touched off a massive, antimilitarist, and antinationalist reaction that brought together anarchist, internationalist, socialist, and pacifist movements under a common cause, which would extend into anti-war resistance during the forthcoming World War.[2]

Milan, one of the hubs of the Milan-Genoa-Turin industrial triangle, was home to a thriving working class and the subsequent leftist

1   Leda Rafanelli, *Leda Rafanelli—Carlo Carrà, Un Romanzo: Arte e Politica in un Incontro Ormai Celebre*, edt. Ciampi Alberto, 60–65.

2   Alessandro Aruffo, *Gli Anarchici Italiani, 1870–1970* (Rome: Datanews, 2010), 105.

associations that accompanied its development throughout Italy. In 1912, the Italian Syndicalist Union (USI, *Unione Sindacale Italiana*) split off from the General Labor Confederation (CGL, *Confederazione Generale del Lavoro*), which had only recently been formed in 1906. The USI distinguished itself by refusing all political affiliations—unlike the CGL's socialist allegiance—and thus its unwillingness to compromise with government or business leaders, giving it a greater revolutionary appeal and higher affinity with pro-organizational anarchists seeking to create large-scale associations. Both the USI and the CGL would remain popular throughout the devastating war, with a combined total of several million members by the advent of fascism.

Tracking back a few years, Leda and her beau Giuseppe Monanni had been invited to Milan in 1908 in order to take over the editorship of the newspaper *The Human Protest* (*La Protesta Umana*) by its directors, Ettore Molinari and Nella Giacomelli. The anarchist newspaper with the largest circulation at that time, *The Human Protest* was published from 1906–1909 and emphasized individual action and rebellion against institutions, going so far as to print articles encouraging readers to occupy the Duomo, Milan's central cathedral.[3] Hence it was no surprise that *The Human Protest* was subject to repeated seizures and the condemnations of its editorial managers, the latest of whom—Massimo Rocca (aka Libero Tancredi), Giovanni Gavilli, and Paolo Schicchi—were having a hard time getting along.

Due to a lack of funding, editorial activity for *The Human Protest* was indefinitely suspended almost as soon as Leda arrived in Milan. She nevertheless became close friends with Nella Giacomelli (1873–1949). Giacomelli had started out as a socialist activist while working as a teacher in the 1890s, but stepped back from political involvement after a failed suicide attempt in 1898, presumably over an unhappy love affair.[4] She then moved to Milan where she met her partner, Ettore Molinari, and turned towards the anarchist movement. Her skepticism, or perhaps burnout, over the ability of humans to foster social change was extended to the anarchist movement, which she later claimed "creates rebels but doesn't make anarchists."[5] Yet she continued on with her literary initiatives and

---

3   Ibid., 11.
4   Ibid.
5   Nella Giacomelli, Anarcopedia, http://ita.anarchopedia.org/ Nella_Giacomelli#cite_ref-permettete_5–0

support of libertarian causes all the same. Her partner Ettore Molinari (1867–1926) was a chemistry teacher at the Polytechnic University. He worked alongside Giacomelli on the newspaper *The Cry of the Masses* (*Il Grido della Folla*, 1902–1907) before launching *The Human Protest*.

Vir had already established Monanni and Leda as leading proponents of individualist anarchism, and they are widely credited for introducing Milanese circles to this new strain of anarchism. There is little consensus among historians as regards precisely how many different currents were present in the Italian anarchist movement from 1900 through WWI: some classify the movement into three camps, which included communist organizers, communist anti-organizers (who favored local, grassroots and spontaneous initiatives over the larger scale and more formal structures of the communist organizers), and individualists; others count no less than six predominant interpretations, which were communist, syndicalist, antimilitarist/pacifist, educationalist/humanitarian, local grassroots groups, and individualist.[6]

Depending on whether their energy was devoted to personal development or rabble-rousing, individualist anarchists could be further divided into two different varieties: those who generally agreed with the ideas of Leda and Monanni, and those who more readily fell in with the likes of Libero Tancredi (1884–1973). Much of the notoriety attributed to individualist anarchists, and perhaps even anarchists in general, can be traced to the attitudes and actions of those who, like Tancredi, advocated a violent, often militaristic form of amoralism; to the detriment of our understanding of the "other" form of individualist anarchism, a more "refined" interpretation of anarchism, meaning more intellectual or, according to its detractors, more elitist and bourgeois.

Individualist anarchism, as Leda and Monanni interpreted it, drew from the conviction that structural changes would not be enough to advance humanity. Only a rigorous examination and adjustment of one's mentality, in order to develop the capacity to think and act as a liberated individual, would truly ensure emancipation from all oppressive institutions. Such examination and adjustment, naturally, could not be mandated or prescribed: it depended solely upon an individual's initiative, though support and encouragement could be provided, particularly through the right kind of reading material. The ultimate goal of an individualist

---

6   Giorgio Sacchetti, *Comunisti contro individualisti, il dibattito sull'organizzazione del 1907*. Bollettino del Museo del Risorgimento, anno XXXV. (Bologna: 1990).

anarchist would be to ensure their own happiness, by living their everyday life in accordance with their authentic self and not bowing down to any form of social or cultural construct that would limit the free expression of their personality and spirit. By and large, individualist anarchists were largely indifferent to whether or not society caught on to their school of thought. As Leda explained: "Individualists feel and advocate a different concept and vision of life, entirely different from other interpretations. And it's truly this different understanding of life that gives us our reason for being and our indifference to proselytism. Whether or not people follow us, whether or not we're understood, we remain what we are and our ideas are not diminished nor devalued, but remain intact, alive inside of us."[7] This "indifference" to proselytism did not mean individualist anarchists would refrain from diffusing their ideas through propaganda, however: "We give everything without expecting anything back—and we don't want anything in exchange for what we give. We release our ideas into the general public, almost sure that they will be lost and scattered, and not only does this fail to bother us, but we also feel somewhat delighted in this useless effort, the effort of giving something to those who refuse it, to those who do not understand the value of the gift."[8]

The "different concept and vision of life" advocated by individualist anarchists provided a stark contrast to the major ethical trends of the mid to late nineteenth century. Altruism was considered to be at the heart of human ethics, as reflected by the works of John Stuart Mill, August Comte, and Arthur Schopenhauer; more equitable distribution of resources amongst ordinary people was a central preoccupation of socialist groups. By the turn of the century, however, a philosophical backlash had risen in the form of staunch individualism, based largely on Nietzsche's celebration of individual freedom, creativity, and capacity for self-transformation outside of the constraints of ordinary morality and social values. Nietzsche's hardline criticism of the state, religion, and social institutions in general was matched in intensity by his disdain for the conformity and mediocrity of the herd mentality, manifested within any type of mass movement or organization. Away from the herd, however, an individual could strive to become an *Übermensch*, a superman: various interpretations exist as to what exactly this superman represents, but it is

---

7   Leda Rafanelli, "La mia libertà" in *La libertà*, 18 October 1913. Fondo "LR-M," conserved at the ABC.

8   Ibid.

generally understood to symbolize a form of greatness, of potential realized, of human skill and intelligence at its finest.

In addition to Nietzsche, Max Stirner (1806–1856) is also credited as a source of inspiration for the individualist current of anarchism. Stirner's work, particularly *The Ego and its Own* (1845), argues against the trappings and conditioning of society and posits the amoral *egoist* as the protagonist of a new form of liberty: "You despise the egoist because he puts the spiritual in the background as compared with the personal, and has his eyes on himself where you would like to see him act to favor an idea."[9] The truly free individual, however, the *unique one*, recognizes no authority, whether in the form of an idea or a person, and experiences an authentic and highly individualistic existence: "I am owner of my might, and I am so when I know myself as unique. In the unique one the owner himself returns into his creative nothing, of which he is born. Every higher essence above me, be it God, be it man, weakens the feeling of my uniqueness, and pales only before the sun of this consciousness."[10]

Aside from laying the foundations for new forms of individualist ideology, the work of these two authors was also used to justify a wide range of amoral and perverse behaviors, including hyper-nationalism, arguments of racial superiority, and general disregard for the rights and freedoms of other people: the idea of being super and above the masses, or unique and unbridled by authority, could be flipped in order to posit the inferiority or insignificance of the masses.

The interpretation of individualist anarchism championed by Libero Tancredi, often called egoist individualism as compared to the altruistic individualism of Leda and Monanni, provides an example of this logic. Anarchism, "is the struggle against humanity, in order for humanity to progress [...] It is responsible and irreverent sacrilege, many times horrific, always misunderstood, and always victorious; more sublime and immortal than any divinity, as it perpetuates throughout the centuries with the ethical and indomitable strength of its will and creed."[11] Through his articles and his lectures, Tancredi urged other anarchists to resort to violence and line their

---

9   Max Stirner, *The Ego and His Own*, trans. Steven Byington, 1907. URL: http://theanarchistlibrary.org/library/max-stirner-the-ego-and-his-own#toc14.

10   Ibid.

11   Libero Tancredi, *L'anarchismo contro l'anarchia* (Pistoia: Casa Editrice "Rinascimento," 1914), 485.

pockets with "holy dynamite,"[12] professing that "respect of the freedom of others is a form of 'self-castration.'"[13] Ultimately aligning with the fascist government, Tancredi was by no means loyal to anarchist principles: yet the "little pimp," as Monanni called him,[14] was loud enough to attract attention to his skewed understanding of the anarchist cause.

The logic of individualist anarchism, as Monanni and Rafanelli understood it, was to dismantle all of the thoughts or beliefs imposed upon a person's psyche through the society and institutions within which they developed, thus freeing them to think for themselves and come to their own conclusions. A person's greatest enemy, according to this reasoning, was not the state or the church, but themselves: an individual, his or herself, was the source of all belief in limitations and legitimization of repression and hierarchy.

Furthermore, under the logic of individualist anarchism, the concept of humanity itself is merely an illusion. Only the individuals that comprise humanity are real entities, and thus rather than work toward improving (or improving conditions for) humanity, one focuses on the individual as both the end and the means for transformation. The happiness of each person has that same person as its own agent; therefore, society must be designed in such a way that everyone has complete freedom to conduct their own personal revolution; for only after liberating oneself can one help others to liberate themselves.

As this theoretical, philosophically-oriented strain of anarchism flourished in the newspapers and magazines Leda and Monanni directed, a larger debate was taking place within the Italian anarchist movement concerning the principle of organization. The June 1907 Italian Anarchist Congress had brought together activists and representatives from across the peninsula to discuss common concerns and initiatives, fueling the continued debate concerning the best methods for fostering revolutionary change. In contrast with the syndicalist, communist, and communist anti-organizational strains of anarchism, the relative indifference of individualists to any form of organization came across, to some observers, as

---

12   Antonioli, M; Berti, G; Fedele, S; Iuso, P (directors), *Dizionario Biografico degli Anarchici Italiani* volume 2, 483.

13   Armando Borghi and Gaetano Salvemini, *Mezzo Secolo di Anarchia (1898– 1945)* (Naples: Edizioni scientifiche italiane, 1954), 78–79.

14   Giorgio Sacchetti, "Comunisti contro individualisti, il dibattito sull'organizzazione del 1907," *Bollettino del Museo del Risorgimento*, anno XXXV, 1990.

smug. Anarchist theorist Saverio Merlino (1856–1930) summed up his observations in a notorious 1907 interview later titled *The End of Anarchism?*: "Currently, the anarchist party [sic] is fragmented by the conflict between the advocates of two different trends; that is, between the individualists and the organizationalists. The organizationalists are unable to find a form of organization compatible with their anarchist principles. The individualists, who are opposed to organization in any form, can't figure out how to act."[15] The general takeaway from Merlino's interview was that socialism had co-opted the best intellectual fruit of the anarchist movement, which now failed to produce any new ideas.

The lively criticism and debate in the anarchist community was a sign of its vitality as well as its lack of coherence. Historian Gino Cerrito describes *The Human Protest* as a perfect microcosm of the myriad and often competing strains of anarchism: "Aside from the voices of anti-organizational, anarcho-communism—which its directors Nella Giacomelli and Ettore Molinari claimed to profess—it was the playground for ideas and trends in the Movement. Therefore, within its pages, one found articles by organizational and anti-organizational anarchists, pieces by individualists inspired by Nietzsche and Sorel, yet [these points of view] were not published as opinions in free competition with one another, but more as components of an undigested minestrone soup, with undetermined colors, to the point that one often wondered if such ideological confusion reflected the theoretical inconsistency and practical incapacity of its editors and directors to present a coherent discourse."[16]

Yet this heterogeneity was later defended in the 1920s by Errico Malatesta, when he noted that "[…] with regard to their moral causes and ultimate ends, individualist anarchism and communist anarchism are the same thing, or nearly the same thing. […] The question, in my opinion, is therefore not between "communists" and "individualists," but between anarchists and non-anarchists."[17]

At any rate, Leda was clear about what her own, personal practice of anarchism consisted of:

---

15 Luigi Galleani, *The End of Anarchism?* trans. Sartin and D'Attilo (Orkney: Cienfuegos Press, 1982).

16 Gino Cerrito, *Dall'insurrezionalismo alla settimana rossa: per una storia dell'anarchismo in Italia 1881–1914* (Florence: CP, 1977), 107.

17 Errico Malatesta, *Rivoluzione e lotta quotidiana* (Venice: Edizioni Antistato, 1982), 211.

We are, by dignity of character, enemies of collective Celebrations, useless demonstrations, *official* Discussions, obstacles to our individual freedom. Only someone with an Anarchist soul and mind feels united to all his brothers and sisters in Ideas, known or unknown, while always remaining free to decide whether or not to come together, or to meet only when it is necessary to exchange Ideas and important tasks. Nobody cares about the personal affairs of their *Compagni*, if they have a family, whether or not they make good money, how they live. All we need is to feel united, close in our minds and in our hearts. Among us, the most *elevated* individual on the social, cultural, economic ladder understands, instructs, and even helps the most *elementary*, the most uneducated and underprivileged of Compagni. One example: Pietro Gori, and a more humble, illiterate *laborer*—who visited while I was staying at Gori's house in Rosignano Marittimo—had a lively discussion on events that now I can't remember. And Pietro listened closely to the Compagno from Pisa who spoke in his rude and colorful dialect and shared his accurate and incisive observations. And in the end Pietro told him: "You've enlightened me."

The young and…not-yet-famous Painter felt magnetized towards us, as we, at that time, new as we were to the Milanese scene, were a little disoriented. We certainly were not *important* figures in the nucleus—as we would become in later years, due to the difficult challenges we all had to overcome.

The Painter would attentively listen to my Compagno who, when he found it necessary to express his Ideas, was truly lucid and interesting. The Painter, perhaps without realizing it, admired him. They were two Individuals with such different temperaments and personalities that they naturally felt the need to externalize their thoughts in open contrast, especially regarding Art and Literature. And it was really this contrast that gave rise to a deep intellectual interest.

My Compagno had a plan that was rather bold, in light of the scarcity of means we all had available to us. His idea was to create the *Casa Editrice Sociale* in order to distribute the best Books written by Our Predecessors, as well as our own Press. He dreamed of publishing a Newspaper, a Magazine, and we would discuss this dream, delighting in thinking about this plan for our work and propaganda which, in those days, seemed almost impossible. He counted on me for a lot, not just in terms of literary collaboration, but for a dispassionate type of labor, as a Typographer, my trade of choice, which in those days I was hired to perform, and paid well to do so, at the Print shop of our Compagno Baraldi.

My Compagno's *dream* was to find an empty warehouse, or even a cellar, and purchase cases of characters (I am a fantastic *composer* with *mobile* characters)—since there was no chance we would be able to purchase a *linotype*—and buy, in installments, a printing machine he knew how to operate. We went on to publish, on a very low budget—since we worked without hopes of profit—not just a Newspaper and a Magazine, but also elementary propaganda Pamphlets for new proselytes, high-quality literary and theoretical Works, and then, many years later, we released *Memoirs of a Revolutionist* by Kropotkin, the writings of Bakunin and the complete works (eleven volumes) of Nietzsche. We published London's Novels and many other interesting works, including *The Ego and Its Own* and *Minor Writings* by Stirner.

My Compagno, back then, did not talk much about his plan, but developed it inside his own head, only discussing the project with the few people He trusted. Already, together, before running off to Milan—sometimes going without food—we had managed to publish *VIR* and a literary magazine that I directed, *The Black Scarf* [*La Sciarpa Nera*].

We were young, intelligent, active and...*uncensored*, but already unpopular with the *forces of Order*, as we were subverters of the Order itself. They couldn't understand us, but they feared us all the same, and during the years to come we would come to understand the violence of a struggle that lasted for decades, and that will always continue, as we will always be different from everyone who gives orders.[18]

---

18   Leda Rafanelli, *Leda Rafanelli—Carlo Carrà, Un Romanzo: Arte e Politica in un Incontro Ormai Celebre,* edt. Alberto Ciampi, 70–72.

***

The convergence of Leda and Monanni's publishing careers would eventually lead to the creation of the great libertarian press they had begun planning as soon as they got to Milan: first called the Libreria Editrice Sociale (Social Publishing Bookstore), their initiative would be put on hold during WWI and then renewed in the 1920s as the Casa Editrice Sociale (Social Publishing House), which, after being shut down in 1926 by the fascists, would be reincarnated one last time as the Casa Editrice Monanni (Monanni Publishing House) from 1927–1933. Over the course of two decades, this original publishing venture would have to overcome massive political and economic turbulence in order to produce and distribute thousands of copies of hundreds of different titles. Yet it succeeded in providing cultural and intellectual resources to the entire anarchist movement, and even found, particularly thanks to its social-based novels, a wide audience amongst the general population. Throughout its evolution and name changes, this publishing house was responsible for bringing many Italians into contact with intellectual currents sweeping through other parts of Europe. Within the practice of individual anarchism, this publishing initiative represented a wholehearted attempt to contribute to the education of readers, regarding their personal liberation and the dismantling of societal institutions, without any expectations for much profit, if any.

Soon after arriving in Milan, Leda edited the new newspaper *The Social Question* (*La Questione Sociale*), a weekly that ran for seven weeks in autumn 1909. She then spearheaded the creation of a new magazine meant to serve as a continuation of *Vir*, called *The Black Scarf*, which lasted for four issues between April 1909 and August 1910 (it was published after the couple moved to Milan—not before, as Leda writes in the excerpt above). Featuring a cover designed by Carlo Carrà, the articles in the first issue of *The Black Scarf* include an Italian translation of *Anarchism and American Traditions* by Voltairine de Cleyre; a translation of Octave Mirbeau's *The Bad Shepherds*, a play about a workers' strike; articles by Leda and Monanni (Monanni writing under the pen name G. Aretino) about law and anticlericalism; and the libretto to Pietro Gori's musical work *Calendimaggio*. The second issue continues with articles on science and religion, "The Divine Spouses" ("Le Spose Divine") by Élie Reclus, book reviews, and continued installments of Mirbeau's and de Cleyre's work.

In 1909, two major solidarity campaigns were underway in Milan: one against the execution of Francisco Ferrer, a Spanish pedagogue who founded the progressive Escuela Moderna for working-class children, then was accused of sedition and summarily executed, and the second against the visit tsar Nicholas II of Russia paid to the king of Italy.[19] The tsar was condemned by the international progressive community due to his penchant for bloody repression and executions of political opponents. Leda adjusted her output accordingly, writing a 500-page novel entitled *Toward Siberia: Scenes of the Russian Revolution* (*Verso la Siberia: Scene della rivoluzione russa*) under the pen name Costantino Bazaroff, "Russian refugee."

Through their continued contributions to other newspapers and magazines, Leda and Monanni were in contact with the majority of the radical network in Northern Italy. In addition to raising her and Monanni's son born in 1910—Marsilio, or Aini, an Arabic nickname which Leda translated as "my eye"—and collaborating with a host of newspapers, Leda would publish eight full-length adult novels over the twenty-five years she spent in Milan, including *Little Star and the Ogress* (*Stellino e l'orchessa*), *Enchantment* (*Incantamento*), *Social Sketches, Hero of the Masses, New Seed, Women and Females, Like a Meteor*, and *The Oasis*.

It took a while for Leda and Monanni's publishing house to get off of the ground. The Libreria Editrice Sociale existed at various addresses in Milan from 1909 until 1914, when WWI broke out. Although a complete catalog has not been preserved, there is evidence that it released at least thirty full-length works—originals and translations—by Pietro Gori, Peter Kropotokin, Max Stirner, Nicola Simon, Francesco Ferrer, Louise Michel, Leo Tolstoy, Octave Mirabeau and Charles Albert. Starting in 1910, it announced a new initiative called the Propaganda and Study Library (*Biblioteca di propaganda e di studio*), a series of low-cost, shorter-format publications that addressed specific aspects of anarchist theory and practice, including titles such as Giovanni Petrini's *Syndicalist practice* and Pietro Gori's *Socialism and Anarchy*. In addition, it issued weekly anarchist periodicals such as *Revolt* (*La Rivolta*) and *Freedom* (*La Libertà*), and even a monthly bibliographic newsletter to keep clients and readers up-to-date on new and forthcoming anarchist releases.

As people caught wind of the Libreria Editrice Sociale's vocation, it gradually became an important distribution center for anarchist publications and subversive publishing in general, although its true potential wouldn't be realized until it was revived as the Casa Editrice Sociale in the

---

19   Pier Carlo Masini, Introduction to Leda Rafanelli, *Una Donna e Mussolini*, 12.

1920s. Complementing her publishing activity, Leda began contributing heavily to other newspapers such as *The Libertarian Woman* (*La Donna Libertaria*) from 1912–1913 and *Forward!* (*Avanti!*), the weekly newspaper of the socialist party directed by Mussolini from 1912 until 1915, when he was fired for breaking with the party line and advocating military intervention in WWI. Leda's articles from her first few years in Milan, at least those that remain in her archived papers, largely focus on explaining individualist anarchism and denouncing military intervention on the African continent. Yet during that period of time, the intense organization and insurrection taking place in Italy was also a major concern in the anarchist community.

From June 7th to June 14th, 1914, popular insurrection spread across the center of Italy following the deaths of three peaceful protesters killed in Ancona, allegedly by carabinieri, at an anti-war/anti-militarism rally.[20] A spontaneous general strike broke out in the city, first rippling through the regions of Tuscany, Le Marche, Emilia Romagna, and then beyond, leading to hosts of local insurrections, popular expropriations, sabotage of railroad networks, and the declaration of provisional governments over the course of the next few days—what came to be known as the *settimana rossa*, or *red week*—as small towns spontaneously declared themselves autonomous republics. Troops were called in, dozens of workers were killed and many more injured, and a popular assembly among socialist, syndicalist, and anarchist leaders finally called an end to the strike on the 13th, though the decision was by no means unanimous. Nevertheless, the week's activity demonstrated the population's capacity to form a revolutionary, anti-state front, a factor that probably was seriously taken into consideration as the Italian government weighed the implications of engaging in the great war. In 1915, Italy reversed its initial stance of neutrality and fought, to the surprise of many, on the side of the Allies, incurring over a million military and civilian casualties, which accounted for an estimated 3.5 percent of its population, before the 1918 armistice.

Like many other young men, Monanni escaped to Switzerland in 1916 in order to avoid conscription, thus putting on hold the publishing activity he and Leda had begun under the Libreria Editrice Sociale. He spent five years in exile, collaborating with French language anarchist and pacifist magazines and newspapers. After being accused and found guilty of participating in a 1918 revolutionary plot in Zurich, he was forced to serve time in prison and only returned to Italy in 1920.

20   Alessandro Aruffo, *Gli Anarchici Italiani, 1870–1970*, 109.

Leda also tried to escape to Switzerland, but her passport was denied because the police, who had dutifully kept her under surveillance since 1908, observed she had been maintaining contact with various draft dodgers.[21] Still in Milan, she met Raffaele Ottolenghi, an orientalist scholar who published a newspaper called *Voices from the Orient* (*Voci di Oriente*) and organized a variety of activities focused on raising awareness of Asian and African cultures, including a solidarity campaign for Ethiopian falashas. Through Ottolenghi, she was introduced to Emmanuel Taamrat (1888–1963), a falasha who had come to Italy from Ethiopia a few years earlier to study at the yeshiva of Florence. He and Leda stayed in very close contact, and from the description of his letters in her memoirs, it appears he was an important source of psychological support during this time, as Leda had to not only handle raising her son alone in the middle of a war, but also the death of her father, in 1916, followed by that of her mother in 1919.

Italy did not get back on its feet after WWI: its economy was in ruins, inflation was skyrocketing, and the rare jobs available offered working conditions as ghastly as the living conditions the average citizen faced in a war-torn country. The years 1919 and 1920 are referred to as the *biennio rosso*, or *red biennial*, a two-year period of constant strikes, pickets, skirmishes and insurrections, in both urban and rural areas. Thousands of strikes broke out nationwide, culminating in the September 1920 occupation of the factories—first ironworks, and then other factories throughout Northern Italy during which workers forcibly ousted the owners and continued production under their own control. Lacking concerted organization, as the insurrection was largely based on local and spontaneous initiatives driven by syndicalists, anarchists, and socialists, the failed revolution and continued economic pressure paved the way for the rise of Mussolini's fascists, who proclaimed a "third way" between revolution and the current government, formally consolidated as a political force to be reckoned with after their 1922 March on Rome.[22]

---

21   Franco Schirone, *Leda Rafanelli. Tra letteratura e anarchia. Atti del convengo*, edt. Fiamma Chessa (Reggio Emilia: Biblioteca Panizzi, 2008), 85.

22   In October 1922, Mussolini's fascists organized a march through Rome, demanding the king of Italy to hand over control of the government, with the intent of taking it by force should he refuse. The king yielded to the pressure and assigned Mussolini the official duty of forming a new government on October 30, thus paving the way for the creation of a fascist state.

The frustration of a devastating war, the impotent state, and a failed revolution created a dire need for dialog and exchange on new perspectives and ways to address these issues. The works of new theorists—philosophers who were still alive and able to make sense of what was going on—not to mention the insights from activists living through the tumultuous times needed to be diffused. Upon Monanni's return from Switzerland, he and Leda revived the initiative begun before WWI under the Libreria Editrice Sociale and reintroduced the publishing house as the Casa Editrice Sociale in 1920. Given their activity during the red biennial, anarchists were considered to be the biggest threat to civil order, by and large denied the right to publicly demonstrate: hence publishing took on an even more important role in diffusing libertarian ideas.[23]

The Casa Editrice Sociale was a leading force in the cultural education of anarchists, as well as broad segments of the population interested in reading novels that addressed current social issues. Its booklist contained hundred of titles, written by Errico Malatesta, Giuseppe Rensi, Giuseppe Ferrari, Luigi Fabbri, Italo Toscani, as well as translations of Karl Marx, Felix Le Dantec, Georges Palante, Charles Darwin, Charles Albert, Eugenio Sue, Nietzsche, and Stirner. Though perhaps only a few of these names are recognized today, the majority of these authors were, in the 1920s, cutting-edge philosophers, revolutionary theorists, and advocates of alternate political systems, many released for the first time in Italian. The Casa Editrice Sociale also supported the launch of a new newspaper, *The Free University* (*L'Università Libera*), one of the last anarchist periodicals to circulate before WWII. Edited by anarchosyndicalist Carlo Molaschi (1886–1953), ten issues of *The Free University* were released in 1925, advocating more solidarity and associationism among individualist anarchists. The magazine was shut down due to continued police persecution, the same reasons that obliged the Casa Editrice Sociale to close its doors in 1926.

In parallel with the myriad developments, setbacks, and divergences in anarchist theory and practice during the first two decades of the twentieth century, a different avant-garde trend was evolving amongst Italian artists: futurism. With its nationalistic overtones, futurism was by default incompatible with anarchist principles, nevertheless the two movements came into frequent contact given their common interest in subverting the status quo.

---

23   Franco Schirone, *Leda Rafanelli. Tra letteratura e anarchia. Atti del convengo*, 87.

***

PASSISTS. Over time, this definition will serve to divide two Artistic trends. We were passists, we merely expected every branch of Art—Literature, Painting, Sculpture, Music—to provide a lively and individual expression of Beauty, Harmony, Truth, as appreciated through the Artist or Creator's liberated personality. The Futurists denied, or at least claimed to deny, the entire Past, all of the works from the Past, saying that nothing was worth the trouble of being preserved; and as new representatives of a new Art they had the duty to abolish Museums, Galleries, Libraries: to replace the old, outdated stuff with their new, original, unscrupulous, futuristic Works. And they called themselves FUTURISTS. Time has shown us how few of their *works* actually replaced the Masterpieces that have been admired for years, for centuries, by people from all over the World!

They would have liked to wipe out the enthusiasm, the admiration, the value given to all the Artists from the glorious Past, from the Greeks to Leonardo, from Caravaggio to Michelangelo, from Canova to Leopardi. The destruction they imagined would not spare Sculpture, nor Painting, nor Poetry, nor Music, nor Literature—the most beloved Artists and writers would be replaced by symbolic and cubist caricatures, paintings without any meaning, impotent attempts at Sculpture, *free-word poetry* instead of Literature—and everything they did not know how to create was sketched out in their brains, drunk on words they didn't even understand were mere contradictions and stupid vainglory. You should have heard them denigrate every work of Art, showing off their patent ignorance of Artists who had gone so far as to sacrifice their Lives for their Art, who renounced the bourgeois lifestyle of earning money, who could not love Art alongside religion.

[…] A few Painters had begun to paint pictures in the new *manner*. One of them—who was already garnering great reviews from the critics for his large-scale compositions—had exhibited his work, a large, lively, colorful impressionistic painting, right before he joined the new School. He had captured a nighttime scene on the canvas, a high-society social hour in an outdoor Café in Paris. Little tables full of Glasses, coffee cups, surrounded by a crowd of night owls and *coquettes* dressed in the fashion of those days: flared skirts, huge hats covered with feathers and flowers, exaggerated décolletages, legs crossed to show off their figures and—in the foreground—a huge fat woman, with a low neckline and an enormous hat bursting with colors, laughing with her mouth open wide. It was the expression of animalistic carefreeness, flesh that takes pleasure obliviously, dazzling colors with a certain pictorial charm. But—once he accepted the *rules* of the new School—the Painter reworked his painting in the new *manner*. He painted dozens of legs in static *movement* between the little tables, he added women's heads above the figures that were already painted, he slathered on different hues in chaotic disorder, and he enlarged the mouth of the woman in the middle to make it look like a red furnace, and titled the painting *The laugh*. But now so confused, botched, spoiled, it didn't make anyone laugh. People looked at it and said: "Will you look at that!" And yet, before it was *updated*, it was actually a lively and original painting.[24]

***

The regressive stance of a "passist" doesn't match up with the progressive views Leda held and promoted throughout her life. Yet her outspoken efforts to distance herself from futurism are just as strong as her efforts to distance herself from egoist individualism. Futurism also advocated violence and militaristic change of society, as well as outspoken misogyny. Retrospectively, its lack of appeal is enhanced by the fact that the majority of its members aligned with the fascist regime in the 1920s.

Filippo Marinetti (1876–1944), born in Alexandria, Egypt and then sent to study in France in his late teens, is by and large considered the founder and leading figure behind futurism in Italy. He singlehandedly pronounced its advent with the *Futurist Manifesto* in February 1909, which achieved notoriety after it was printed by *Le Figaro*, a

---

24   Leda Rafanelli, *Leda Rafanelli—Carlo Carrà, Un Romanzo: Arte e Politica in un Incontro Ormai Celebre*, edt. Alberto Ciampi, 85–91.

mainstream French newspaper still in circulation today. Preceding the dada movement by a few years, and Bréton's surrealist manifestos by fifteen years, futurism is considered to be the most prominent (and perhaps only) homegrown avant-garde artistic movement of twentieth-century Italy. Its disdain for everything old, classic, or in any way associated with the past was matched by its reverence for youth, power, and technology. It can easily be considered an artistic byproduct of the Industrial Revolution.

In 1909, Marinetti called for a rupture with all traditional standards of beauty, and the foundation of a new culture built on the glorification of violence and speed. His manifesto reflects an aggressive, hyper-macho vision of the world, stating in point 9: "We want to glorify war—the only way to cleanse the world—militarism, patriotism, the destructive gestures of libertarians, the beautiful ideas people die for, and contempt for woman."[25] He ends his appeal with the founding of the new movement: "From Italy, we launch our manifesto of incendiary and devastating violence to the world, through which, today, we establish FUTURISM, because we want to liberate this country from its fetid gangrene of professors, archeologists, tourists guides and antiquarians. For too long Italy has been a flea market. We want to liberate it from the numerous museums that cover the land with their cemeteries."[26] Yet Marinetti's advocacy of social change was little more than a veiled excuse for rowdiness, leading one scholar to note: "Even if [Marinetti] spoke of revolution, his attention was focused on the phenomenon of violence, violence in and of itself, not revolutionary violence."[27] Whenever Leda mentions Marinetti in her writings, she refers to him as the "bald millionaire"—alluding to his bourgeois lifestyle and hair issues—deeming his real name too worthless to be reproduced.

In 1911, Carlo Carrà completed a painting, *The anarchist Galli's funeral* (*I funerali dell'anarchico Galli*) considered to be one of the most representative futurist works, as it coherently translates these new philosophical lines into visual art. The painting, which made Carrà's name known in national and international artistic circles, conveys a frantic

25 Marinetti, Filippo, *Manifesto del futurismo*.
26 Ibid.
27 Laura Iotti, "Futuristi e anarchici: Dalla fondazione del futurismo all'ingresso italiano nella prima guerra mondiale (1909–1915)," *Carte Italiane*, Series 2, Vol. 6, 2010.

succession of figures and outlines, sharp brush strokes and geometric, linear patterns in predominantly red and orange tones, save for a break of blue and green tones in the sky area. The subject of the painting, Angelo Galli, was an anarchist killed by police during a 1904 strike in Milan: his funeral had given rise to another clash between anarchists and police.

As evidenced by Carrà's contributions of graphics to several anarchist newspapers, including *The Black Scarf*, not to mention his logo design for the *Libreria Editrice Sociale,* there was, despite the discrepancy concerning futurism's nationalism and anarchism's anti-statism, a degree of crossover between the anarchist and futurist movements. In certain aspects, the energy behind futurism was similar to that behind anarchism: free, creative, and subversive. Most importantly, both futurism and anarchism took a strong, critical stance against continuing the bourgeois social and political institutions of the past, an aspect Leda nevertheless subverts in her later writings by claiming she is and always was a "passist."

In 1912, journalist Renzo Provinciali (1895–1981) published a manifesto called *Futurism and Anarchism*, often interpreted as an attack against Marinetti, in *The Barricade (La Barricata)*, a Parma-based newspaper that became a rallying point for anarchist-futurists. Provinciali declared: "Anarchists have always been deeply futurist, and they will understand the compelling need to go deep into the Futurist ideal, true Futurism, Futurism free from dictatorship and ambition, and thus anarchists will become even more perfect, even more aware of the political and artistic responsibilities. Thus futurist-anarchists and anarchist-futurists, two ideals, two classes of people who mutually complete one another."[28]

The motivation to meld the anarchist and futurist movements mirrored a desire to strengthen the avant-garde: anarchists were considered the ideological (political or social) avant-garde, whereas futurists were considered the artistic (visual and literary) avant-garde. Mutually they could, theoretically, facilitate the revolution: the argument often advanced was that an anarchist society would need new, hence futurist, art, and futurist art would need open-minded, hence free and anarchist, minds in order to appreciate it.

Marinetti, too, saw the potential for strength in numbers and even wrote a manifesto in 1910 entitled *Our common enemies (I nostri nemici comuni)* inviting anarchist and syndicalist groups to join the futurists in

---

28   Renzo Provinciali, "Futurismo e Anarchia," *La Barricata*, number 1, May 1912.

fighting political and cultural passatism.[29] However, Marinetti's efforts to court the revolutionary left were largely in vain, and he eventually turned toward the idea of developing the futurist movement independently, going so far as to write a constitution for a Futurist Political Party in 1918. In 1919, the nascent party gave up its own political agenda and blended in with Mussolini's proto-fascist party. Not all futurists followed Marinetti's lead, but many did, fearing the repercussions of rebelling against the status quo, ironically enough.

***

And so, the Artists of the Future—captained by the bald millionaire—sprung into action. Not just in the field of Painting, but also Literature—with the famous *free-word poetry*, which drove the Typographers crazy as they were forced to compose type in different fonts all on the same line: not just nonsensical words, but text that began with font 6 characters (and only people who've worked as composers in a Print shop can understand this tiring extravagance) and finished in the font used for posters. And after Literature—first demolished with all of its millennial representatives and then created anew with futurist poems, verses, and books—after Literature came Music, which was uprooted along with its classic instruments—pianos, violins, guitars, cellos—"ridiculous instruments that already belong to the Past," and performed (if you can call it performance) by *masters* of the new School, who today nobody remembers the names of. And it was actually the seraphic Painter R. who devised the first instrument of Futurist Music, pompously baptized as the "NOISE-INTONER," which made its debut on the stage of the Teatro Lirico in Milan one unforgettable evening that remains only in the memories of those who were there, since, *once the party's over*, sometimes all that's left is the smoke. This event was preceded by another Manifesto full of the usual contempt for Music from the greatest and most renowned Masters, music that needed to be eradicated by the new art.

---

29 Laura Iotti, "Futuristi e anarchici: Dalla fondazione del futurismo all'ingresso italiano nella prima guerra mondiale (1909–1915)."

That evening, the Teatro Lirico was packed. The Futurists stood together in a dense group on the stage, anticipating the usual reactions. Audience members and journalists discussed their different theories on what the Concert would be like, and what this single instrument, which was completely new (different, evidently, from the old instruments) had to accomplish. And the Galleries were crowded with masses of dissidents—the real fans of Lyrical Music, who would attend every show and Concert, crammed together and uncomfortable in their seats yet detached from everything, aware only of the charm of the harmonious waves that surrounded them, ecstatic when they heard the voices of their favorite singers. That evening, as we waited for whatever the new Masters were going to show us, as soon as the *huckster* appeared among his disciples, a chorus of yells, applause, and whistles immediately exploded, which foreshadowed what was going to happen that evening. And it was very difficult for the announcer to get everyone to quiet down. As he made derogatory statements about past and contemporary Musicians, the names of these same beloved, admired Masters fell from the Gallery like pebbles, each according to individual preferences: "Wagner!" "Verdi!" "Beethoven!" "Chopin!" as well as the titles of their famous works. Yet the Leader of the Futurists responded to mentions of these names with gestures of disdain, as if he wanted to distance himself from a swarm of annoying, insistent insects.

But when he announced we would finally see this *unique instrument*, which was supposed to represent, all by itself, the sum of all instruments from the Past and the Present—from pianos to violins to flutes and trumpets—everyone fell silent. We noticed a rustling from behind the wings, and with screeching wheels, the much-lauded Noise-Intoner appeared on the stage. There was an explosion of shouts, whistles, yells, insults, laughs, while—without anyone understanding a single thing he said—the Leader waved his arms and shouted for silence. You could see his mouth open and close without hearing a word, and the futurist *troupe* cheered, while a plebeian voice from the Gallery shouted at the top

of his lungs: "The grindstone! The grindstone!"—with the
familiar cadence of the itinerant knife-grinders who would
call that word out while walking through the streets in the
outskirts of Milan.

Indeed, if an enemy of the proponents of Futurism had
wanted to mock their attempts at futuristic musical technology by presenting some new instrument, he couldn't
have invented anything more ridiculous or more grotesque
than that trestle of wood with vertical wheels that really did
have an exaggerated likeness to a knife grinder's cart, with
a grindstone and foot-powered belts. Amid the growing
turmoil in the audience, a few voices yelled out: "So let's
have a listen, then! You have to show us what it's supposed to
do!" and, without a word, the poor Painter R., a makeshift
musician, made an obvious effort to turn the wooden wheels.
And with a sharp, irritating screech—which, if compared
to a thundering Wagnerian flood, only had the volume of
a mosquito's buzz—the unheard *concert* began, a concert
that would never be repeated, as the *noise-intoner* was never
presented in another City, and there was nothing more ever
said about it. But, as the wooden wheels turned, producing
shrill and discordant sounds, there was an almost fearsome
reaction from the Audience, and various projectiles began to
fall onto the stage, first happily welcomed by the Leader—
who began to peel an orange that fell near Him—but then
received apprehensively by those present in the front of the
Audience, as now pieces of wood and stones began to fly, and
not all of them reached the stage. Suddenly, from high up,
a chair sailed through the air. Then we left, carrying with us
the image of the Painter R., who in protest had turned those
outlandish wheels against the pieces of sheet metal but could
not, however, overpower the clamor in the slightest. The
Futurists who had maintained their distance from the fracas
were lucky, since small groups representing different ideological trends also came to blows.

I am neither a connoisseur nor a fan of classical Music, but
even someone who only listens to street music produced by
old-fashioned hand-cranked *organs* could understand what a

failure that grotesque attempt by a bunch of imbeciles trying to put on a performance was.[30]

***

Leda overtly distanced herself, and her practice of individualist anarchism, from both futurism and the egoist interpretation of individual anarchism, and for similar reasons in both cases: the emphasis on violence and agitation with little moral justification, as well as the macho posturing and proclamations covering a lack of true intellectual development. Yet such raucous voices tend to be better preserved on the historical record, and thus an understanding of what individual anarchism posits is still somewhat overshadowed by the legacy of those who used it as an excuse to act violently and infringe upon the freedom of others.

---

30   Leda Rafanelli, *Leda Rafanelli—Carlo Carrà, Un Romanzo: Arte e Politica in un Incontro Ormai Celebre,* edt. Alberto Ciampi, 108–115.

CHAPTER VII
Subverting Fascism Through Fiction

"What do you want from these people, then? European Nations need prey, and that's fine. There's no cure for that. It has always been that way: whoever has the brute force of weapons prevails over all others, and when a Nation sends soldiers and cannons to a far away land, it naturally doesn't think about the well-being or freedom of the people it wants to blatantly dominate. Everyone knows this: but what I vehemently reject is the hypocrisy of the intellectual propagandists. You want to make your readers believe that these people bow down joyfully under the yoke, that every new law enthuses them, that your mere presence incites them to work, to bustle about, to fall in line with your views. You know very well that this is not the case, and so you oppress them, you want them to occupy themselves by serving your desires, you insist that they accept your values that you deem to be more civil, which are geared toward just one objective: to exploit all of the wealth of the Colonies, and to subjugate the souls of the indigenous. And I think this is monstrous for free spirits: the indigenous people of Tunisia do not ask France for anything. Most disregard the fact that it exists, along with its past, history, glories and people, and they live very well despite their ignorance. As for us, France has won the liberty to "protect" Tunisia and Algeria. Now tell me, in all sincerity, who has something to gain out of this arrangement? The "protected" or the "protectors?" It goes without saying that if I was English, I would say the same thing looking at the situation in Egypt, India, and the rest. All of the *civilized* world has but a single law: the law of liberticidal domination.

...[yet] I will only speak with you, an intellectual, a colonial propagandist, about your work. I know that all those who come here to do what you do fatten their imaginations with the beauty of everything they see, they go into raptures, as if they only saw these things due to their own virtue. As I've already told you, I've read almost all of the colonial literature, a literature that depicts a people subjugated by force, on their knees and in awe, while I know full well that, in reality, the people are gnawing away at the reins. They only put up with this because the purest form of fatalism guides their thoughts and leads them to patiently wait for their time to come. You can admire the customs and traditions of these people all you want, but you also know that not a single one of these indigenous people—even the poorest and the most ignorant person—will admire or envy anything you own. Everything that you, the European, the "protector," import here, peacefully or forcefully, whether a tax to be paid or the commitment to build a road, even the lavish palaces you erect in the city, everything, believe me, is viewed by the native people with the highest contempt, or at least complete indifference if they are not directly affected by it. What does it matter to them if Tunis starts to look like a European metropolis? The Arabs will take refuge in their own neighborhood, as they do in Cairo, in Istanbul, in Ceylon. The native person, subjugated, leaves you alone to do what you must, but does not care about you, much less admire you. And if, never mind what they want, you mix them up in your business, if you force them to work, to do something new or to understand something unusual, do you really believe that this will cause them to assimilate into your culture? That they will happily work for you? That they will admire you? Never! They are like a drop of oil shaken in a glass of water: even if it dissolves into thousands and thousands of parts, it will all come together, complete and whole, free of any other influence: you want to shake it up, mix it together! It remains a drop of oil in the water![1]

1   Leda Rafanelli (Etienne Gamalier), *L'Oasi*, 187–190.

***

In a philosophical face-off that lasts for ninety pages, interrupted only for the necessary coffee breaks and sessions of individual reflection under the desert sky, Henry Nattier, a French citizen and writer of propaganda in support of Europe's imperialistic campaigns in North Africa, is curtly put in his place by Francois Marcel, a fellow expat who's followed an entirely different path since moving to Tunisia.

Francois, now known as Sidi-el-Kerim, has converted to Islam and given up his professional medical practice to live in accordance with the ancient codes and mores of the Bedouins. Henry, still known as Henry, has fallen in love with the exotic landscapes and women, but hasn't given up his Eurocentric superiority complex or culture, though he does placate his girlfriend Gamra by promising he'll convert to Islam "soon." The two men represent divergent courses of action a citizen of a colonizing nation might take in a conquered land, a juxtaposition of humility and arrogance. In the end, the author's point is made exhaustingly clear: colonial motivations are devoid of merit and altruism, despite their colorful packaging in moral duty and missionary vocation.

The Oasis, by Etienne Gamalier, was published by the Casa Editrice Monanni, the latest reincarnation of the Casa Editrice Sociale, in 1929. The novel's publication coincided with the fascist government's revamped initiative to expand the "Italian Empire." Mussolini, now firmly in power and eager to flaunt his military prowess, made claims to most territories bordering the country or within sailing distance, including Dalmatia, Corsica, Slovenia, and southern regions of Switzerland and France. In an attempt to destroy the resistance movement in colonial Libya, he instituted a "pacification" campaign in 1928, which would cause hundreds of thousands of deaths among indigenous Libyans before the rebel leader Mukhtar was killed in 1931, when the Italian forces declared victory. Of all ironies, Mussolini had been jailed in 1911 for protesting Italian military interference in Libya, but since his swing from left to right, he no longer saw anything wrong with the imperialistic wars he had denounced in the past.

As the former director of the socialist newspaper *Forward!*, Mussolini fully understood the need to sell his point of view to the general population. Almost immediately after rising to power, he issued two laws to facilitate the eradication of any kind of press that objected to or criticized the fascist regime. Decree Law 2 of July 5th 1923 gave local prefect officials the power to press charges against directors of newspapers or periodicals that printed material considered to be capable of breaching the peace, arousing class hatred, or inciting disobedience to the laws.[2] Through the Ministerial Decree of August 9th, 1923, the Press Agency was placed under the control of the Prime Minister—Mussolini himself—who made sure that almost all of the press in Italy was read and controlled.[3] Thus, by 1929 the fascist censors had managed to create a tight system to control and punish Italian newspaper and magazine publishers, effectively stamping out a large number of radical periodicals and, therefore, forums for dissidence against the new regime.

A few moderate voices had the courage to speak out against this. Luigi Albertini (1871–1941), who served as a senator from 1914–1922, remarked: "Today, the press is reduced to only reporting what the government and its prefects allow, as was the case during the War [World I]. Except now it's worse: because during the war, censorship was correctly implemented, and the censor followed the almost always obvious criteria issued by the Ministry of the Interior. This is not the case today: things are randomly sequestered, not by criteria related to a general political interest, but by criteria inspired by personal "considerations" and needs."[4]

In 1923, the Viale Monza site of the Casa Editrice Sociale was destroyed by a police raid and temporarily closed down.[5] Piles of books and papers were burned in the street, and the Casa Editrice Sociale was officially forbidden from printing anarchist literature. Nevertheless, the publishing house limped ahead for another few years, before definitively closing its doors after another police raid in 1926.[6] Yet Leda and Monanni were not thwarted: they restarted the initiative under the name of the Casa Editrice Monanni, continuing the same editorial line, though perhaps more muted, from 1927 through 1933, when their personal and professional relationship dissolved.

The Casa Editrice Monanni released a combination of fiction based on social issues and volumes of philosophy, although Leda and Monanni

2   Maurizio Cesari, *La Censura nel periodo fascista* (Naples: Liguori Editore, 1978).
3   Ibid.
4   Ibid.
5   Franco Schirone, *Leda Rafanelli. Tra letteratura e anarchia. Atti del convengo*, 89.
6   Ibid., 91.

no longer overtly branded their output as anarchist or even radical, so as not to tip off the censors. The Casa Editrice Monanni is credited with introducing the Italian public to translations of groundbreaking work in social theory, including the complete works of Nietzsche, introduced and indexed by his sister Elisabeth Forster-Nietzsche. Other nonfiction releases included the first Italian editions of *The Crowd: A Study of the Popular Mind* by Gustave Le Bon, *The Mystery of Jesus* by Paul-Louis Couchoud, and both volumes of *The History of Materialism* by Federico Alberto Lange, as well as new works by Italian authors, such as *National Syndicalism* by Ezio Maria Olivetti and *Capital and Wages* by Antonio Graziadei. It does not appear as if the Casa Editrice Monanni released any flagrantly anarchist work, or books by well-known anarchist authors: however, we are only aware of the catalog that the publishing house printed and advertised publicly, and we have no idea of what it did or diffused in secret.

The Casa Editrice Monanni directed a large amount of its activity to issuing or reissuing—building upon demand first created by the Casa Editrice Sociale—about a hundred novels, many in Italian translation for the first time, by authors including Maxim Gorky, Jack London, Upton Sinclair, Guy de Teramond, George Bernard Shaw, Aldous Huxley, and thirty-five volumes by P.G. Wodehouse. It supplied books to outlets in Italy and around Europe, including libraries run by the fascist party itself, in addition to radical readers, who, often in prison or exile, would find moral support in reading books that reflected similar sentiments regarding and parallel observations of modern society.

Despite the occasional raids and ever-present surveillance, the reason why the Casa Editrice Monanni was able to print and distribute so much radical material is because it placed a high emphasis on subversive fiction. Fascist censors did not have, and would never develop, the ability to monitor novels: they were more accustomed to looking for short pamphlets or newspapers with splashy titles such as "Down with the Regime!" The government employees who did the actual reading, for the purposes of deciding whether or not a work could be allowed to continue circulating among Italian readers, were actually police officers. Most of these police officers had neither the time to read lots of novels, cover to cover, nor the ability to pick up on subtleties or irony. Thus they were largely unprepared and incapable of weeding out the books that carried radical perspectives or subtle messages, particularly if these books were written under the names of authors who were not already on their radar.

This does not mean, however, that the fascist regime was unaware of the subversive nature of these works of fiction. The Ministry of Propaganda did include a special division to analyze all Italian books in circulation, yet before its creation in 1935, the best the government could do was occasionally monitor the odd novel.

Within this context, publishing translations of books written by unknown foreign authors provided another layer of protection from the censors. If the book was by chance flagged, the publisher would be absolved of any liability for the critical viewpoints therein presented, as the ideology wasn't produced locally by any Italian who could then be promptly arrested. Indeed, the story of *The Oasis* was set in Tunisia, a French "protectorate", rather than Libya or Ethiopia, where the Italian imperialistic forces had been hard at work. If readers were to draw parallels between the two colonial campaigns, the Casa Editrice Monanni could not be blamed for their imaginative prowess.

The publisher's preface reads:

> Etienne Gamalier's *The Oasis* holds a special place in French
> colonial literature. The author has very unique ideas regarding
> colonies and populations subjected to European domination.
> He does not repeat the usual themes of official literature. Cap-
> tivated by the peculiar charm of countries and people of color,
> he seeks to bring to light the ingenuity and sincerity of their
> lifestyles and passions. As is the case with the rest of his work,
> Etienne Gamalier does not attempt to disguise his point of
> view, the result of thorough research and warm sympathy. He
> considers the East—and Africa and Egypt in particular—the
> only land where the adventure of life can unfold in complete
> freedom. All of the problems of European Civilization are
> foreign to these lands. We are pleased to offer our readers *The
> Oasis*, a true novel full of emotion and passion. Other works
> will soon follow in this Collection.[7]

Etienne Gamalier is, of course, one of Leda's pseudonyms, and chances are the same Etienne wrote this preface as well. *The Oasis* can be called a pseudotranslation, which is slightly different from a work simply written under a pen name, as it uses translation to entirely displace

---

7   Leda Rafanelli (Etienne Gamalier), *L'Oasi*, 7.

Subverting Fascism Through Fiction • 145

responsibility for the messages conveyed to a source outside the culture in which the translation is released. Given the increasingly totalitarian state, Leda no doubt understood that the stakes had risen for dissidents, and she adjusted her diffusion strategies accordingly. Sometime in the 1930s, Leda started a "translation" of another book by Etienne Gamalier, entitled Djali the Sheikha (*Djali-La Sceikka*), but was unable to complete more than fifty pages.

The fascists would go on to create their own ad hoc editorial line, with the idea of communicating an official version of "reality" to the Italian public. The Press Office issued several odd dictates to its organs in the 1930s, including directions in 1932 to not talk too much about any episodes of bad weather in Italy, and to not "use foreign words, especially titles...and don't publish novellas by foreign authors." The same office also issued a ban of Christmas trees, for reasons that are not entirely clear.[8]

Leda and Benito Mussolini had previously been acquainted and, although we lack overt confirmation, it is generally assumed that they were romantically involved. As evidenced by the book released by Rizzoli under Leda's authorship in 1946, *A Woman and Mussolini* (*Una Donna e Mussolini*), she and Mussolini saw each other frequently and maintained epistolary correspondence for several years: around forty-five of the letters he sent to her are printed in the book, the first from March 19, 1913 and the last dated October 7, 1914, interspersed with Leda's commentary on the man behind the machine. The letters serve as follow-ups to conversations held in person and provide insight into Mussolini's ideological and philosophical development during the period right before WWI, particularly his ambiguity over the state's involvement in the upcoming war. The official line of the socialists, his party and employer, was non-interventionism, yet Mussolini was already displaying signs of a different conviction entirely.

Leda had met Mussolini as his fame among socialists was beginning to grow. Mussolini had taken over as director of the newspaper *Forward!* in 1912, and his public profile grew thanks to his skills as a competent journalist, a convincing orator, a "new-wave" demagogue and, most importantly, an actor.[9] The published epistolary dialogue between the two activists largely unfolds in the events leading up to the 1914 *settimana*

---

8   Maurizio Cesari, *La Censura nel periodo fascista.*
9   Pier Carlo Masini, Introduction to Leda Rafanelli, *Una Donna e Mussolini*, 19–20.

rossa, for which Mussolini organized meetings and published articles in support of the insurrection.

Mussolini was a fan of Leda's work: in a 1914 letter, he requests that she send him a copy of one of her pamphlets, *Down with the War* (*Abbasso la Guerra*),[10] of which thousands of copies had already been printed and distributed. In her own personal mementos, she kept a copy of this pamphlet and wrote over it: "Pamphlet read and approved, in full, by my friend at the time BM who later became a *guerrista* (warmonger) and later a fascist, head of the government for twenty-five years and then killed by glorious partisans."[11]

The relationship came to an end in 1914, by Leda's account, after she realized that Mussolini was already romantically involved with another woman, and consequently was not as "free as the air" as he had previously claimed to be.[12] Yet their friendship had already started to dissolve as Mussolini moved from the standard socialist ideology to a pro-interventionist, proto-nationalist stance, prompting her to write: "Think about it: it's as if you were Europe and I was Africa. Europe yearns to conquer the free Equatorial lands, but it desires these lands in order to oppress them, exploit them, adapt them to its own lifestyles, to its irrational, false, incorrect, and so-called "civil" lifestyle. Heathen Africa lives its own pure, instinctive, natural, spontaneous life."[13]

Mussolini's understanding of the anarchist movement, however, seems to have been motivated by what he saw at the extreme ends of the scale, focusing on the aberrant, amoral egoism promoted by the likes of Libero Tancredi: "Inside every anarchist there's a failed dictator," Mussolini once professed in an interview with Emil Ludwig.[14] Mussolini went on to found his own movement, the Italian Combat Leagues (Fasci italiani di combattimento) in 1919, which later transformed into the National Fascist Party, making a clean break from socialism by following an ideology based on corporatism: heavy state control and collusion with private corporations in order to reduce conflict and opposition amongst the masses.

---

10 Ibid., 161.
11 Leda Rafanelli, *Abbasso la Guerra*, 1914. Fondo "LR-M" conserved at the ABC.
12 Leda Rafanelli, *Una Donna e Mussolini*, 94–95.
13 Ibid., 148.
14 Ibid., 16.

Given his penchant for tight control over the press and the diffusion of information in general, Mussolini was, once in power, somewhat concerned about the letters he had written as a young man, revealing his vulnerabilities and insecurities, being released to the public. Monanni writes that Mussolini had ordered Leda to destroy these letters, but she refused, and it is probable that the 1923 and 1926 raids on the Casa Editrice Sociale had actually been attempts by Mussolini's officers to find and destroy these letters at any cost.[15] The letters, however, had been safely stored and even transcribed into multiple copies, one of which remained in Monanni's hands when he started working with Rizzoli after WWII.

Mussolini made his way into Leda's fiction, and he is clearly the inspiration for the European character in a short story, *The Water Diviner* (*Il Rabdomante*), published in 1914 in the newspaper *Freedom* (*La Libertà*). The theme of *The Water Diviner* would later be reprised and expanded in a novel, *Enchantment* (*Incantamento*), which she published under the pseudonym Sahara, in 1921. Both pieces paint a portrait of a macho and ambitious man who is nonetheless the victim of his own weaknesses. It almost appears as if the author still has a bit of sympathy for him:

> "I know that we will never be able to understand one another. I love the crazy race, the changing variety of things and moods. I am a slave only to my sensuality. And while I understand that women exploit me and treat me as an instrument of pleasure, I withstand it because I seek emotions, I seek sensations with frenzied anxiety. And as soon as I possess something I desire something new, and I delight in destroying what I first desired. I follow new dreams until I get to the final conquest, and in that fleeting moment I taste its sweetness or bitterness. And then I destroy again, tasting joy and pain. Even with the most ardent love, I can feel the chill of its end and the concealed falseness. Now, again, I'm looking for something new. I follow the desire to stand out among men, to love, to be loved and worshipped, until I feel the pang to make my new lover suffer. All of this just to feel new emotions, because I'm a skeptic, a cynic who never believes in the faith I profess. I mix in with the crowd of classes that I battle in order to divide their favors, and I so love the

15   Franco Schirone, *Leda Rafanelli. Tra letteratura e anarchia. Atti del convengo*, 97.

fiction that I adapt myself to their fashions in order to better blend in amongst those whom I call enemies. You are one of the few who I believe to be my friend, and you told me—audaciously—that you understand me. I don't believe it. But let me ask you one thing—in your opinion—what should I do to find new joy again. Where can I find sensations that are even more intense? I think you're wise, strong, philosophical only because you're indifferent. But I scorn not only indifference, but also prudent wisdom. I disdain the force that understands how to triumph over one's passions—which are so pleasant to surrender to—and I mock the empty, cold philosophy that is born only to give life to another theory that challenges it. So tell me what you think."

So said the European, a modern man, whom life had lavished with gifts and who still enjoyed his youth. An Arab listened, a man of the same age who had nothing and shivered, during that grey European spring, next to a brazier that he fed with grains of incense.

The European had the high brow of a dominator, a direct and bold gaze, brusque gestures, quivering nerves, and seemed to express his strength with every gesture, in every word, while his soul was weak and uncertain.[16] The other, listless and feeble, wrapped in the folds of his traditional clothing, was sitting on the ground, his gestures slow, his words sparse, his gaze intent. He had a strong soul underneath his weak appearance.

"You won't understand me, my brother, so I might as well talk to you in my own language. What are you looking for? You're not sure yourself. What more do you desire? You already have everything a man like you could want."

"I don't have everything. Besides, my desire is infinite and renews itself after every accomplishment."

"So then let all of your desires remain desires."

"I love to fulfill them."

"But when all of your desires are satisfied, what are you left with? Nothing."

---

16 "*While his soul was weak and uncertain*" was added, in Leda's handwriting, to her personal copy of the article printed in *La Libertà*.

"Right. But I still search."

"You can find what you want, but you'll have nothing left afterwards. Because what you have gained will mean nothing to you."

"So then what?"

"Stop searching."

"You mean commit suicide?"

"No. Live. Life offers the deepest sensations, the most exquisite emotions to people who *do not seek them*. Doesn't it seem useless to say: *I want to find a new love—I want to be a genius artist.* Love makes you a slave when you least expect it, and a genius doesn't even know he's a genius."

"But I have to live my life and enjoy it! I want to enjoy living."

"How do you know your life is meant to be full of pleasure? It could be a painful life and you can't change that only by your will. It's not *your* life that you want to live, really, but an artificial life, by trying to force your destiny."

"I want to be happy, I want to be loved, I want to love, I want to be satisfied with myself and my search. But I'm never satisfied."

"Because you deceive yourself."

"What should I do?"

"Nothing."

"But I'm thirsty, thirsty, thirsty! And I can't find a source that can satiate this incredible, spasmodic thirst. I abandon myself to love, I lavish myself in pleasure, I let myself become overwhelmed by events, I get excited, I move, shout, laugh; I destroy the serenity of the woman who loves me, I disdain those who admire me, so I can seek out new admirers, so I can follow everyone else's females. But I only become drunk, my thirst is never quenched..."

"You offer your lips to cups that contain wicked alcohol, and you don't drink the pure water from the source."

"If I could only find that source! Does it exist? Where! Can it slake the thirst of someone who has already drunk too much?"

"Maybe not. But it does exist. And it is clear and pure as the eyes and souls of children, sweet as the juice of dates and the kisses of a faithful woman. It's as fresh as youth, with the fragrance of benzoin. Seek it and kneel down to drink it from the palm of your hand."

"If I searched for it I think I'd find the poison of lips that lie to me, the false love of women that exploit my youth, the sycophantic words of a fake friend. Besides, I'd have to waste my time searching for a while, and I'm really in a hurry, I need to run, for behind me screams an implacable pack of concerns that torment me, a modern man."[17]

***

Mussolini's ascent to power and colonial campaigns certainly inspired Leda as she worked on *The Oasis*. Pro-colonial Henry does not come across as sensual enough to be another veiled representation of Mussolini, yet Jeanne, a French-born woman who has also found a new life in Tunisia, is obviously Leda's alter-ego. Tomboyish and plainly dressed, with short grey hair and dark, piercing eyes, Jeanne has comfortably integrated into the Bedouin culture and now spends her time riding her horse around the desert and assisting the locals during medical emergencies (like her friend Sidi-el-Kerim, she must also have had some sort of health-care training). Having abandoned her bourgeois lifestyle in Paris, after discovering her ex-fiancé was only interested in her for money, she, too, is quick to denounce the falsities and frivolousness of European culture.

Gamra, however, is the only main character native to Tunisia. Her Bedouin family turned their backs on her once she took up with her boyfriend Henry, and the narrative shifts from intellectual discussions on colonialism to the psychological effects of colonialism on a woman in love. Gamra's adoration for Henry is expressed as servitude, which he fully enjoys whenever he's not off sleeping with the wife of a French colonel who lives down the street. Suspicious, Gamra spends her time trying to understand her fate, with the assistance of the local fortune teller Mabruka, who accurately predicts blood, tears, and disaster. Secretly reuniting with a cousin, Gamra confides her fears and anxieties over her relationship with this European man, and her cousin decides to tell her what she thinks is the big difference between the Bedouins and the *Rumi*:

---

17   Leda Rafanelli, "Il Rabdomante," *La Libertà*, 1914. Fondo "LR-MM-MLF" conserved at the ABC.

Before Sidi Jussuf made me his second wife, I was a wash-
erwoman in Tunis, and I went to work in the houses of the
foreigners who lived in the city of the rulers. I met many
madames, I always listened to their words and I know almost
everything the *Rumi* say to glorify the ways they live in their
land. They would talk about everything while I was there,
freely, thinking I couldn't understand their conversations.
However, I speak French rather well and understand it perfectly, as I have always served in the houses of the French. I've
only made the choice to go back and help my husband with
the painful farm work or take care of the house and children
alongside his first wife when I couldn't listen to them any-
more, or watch what the *Rumi* were doing, without wanting
to eat my liver out of rage. But this isn't what I wanted to tell
you, my lady: I wanted to tell you that everything they say,
even about their women and love, is a lie. It is not true that
the *Rumi* only love one wife. Almost all of them, especially if
they're rich, have another wife, or a concubine as the case may
be, who is always kept better, with more love and gifts, than
the first wife. Only they don't keep their women together,
and many times the first wife doesn't know that her mister
is keeping another woman and actually loves the other one
more. It is absolutely not true that they respect their women,
even if they only have one; while they let the women talk
about anything, and sometimes get involved in their affairs,
they then scold the women, and ignore them, acting if they
were just chattering children. And, for their part, the women
do not love their husbands better or more than we love ours.
It is true, they have the freedom to leave the house, even
alone, whenever they want to, but then most of them go out
to meet their lovers. In other lands there are also husbands
who kill their spouses for adultery. It is not true that the
Rumi do not make their women work: the poor women work
just as we work, and not just under the command of their
master, but under the command of unknown rulers, in closed
places called "factories." Virgin maidens are as free as married
women, they go out unescorted to chat with men, pretending
that they don't know anything. Many rich families offer a lot

of money and jewels to a man just so he'll take away a virgin daughter, a sign that she means nothing, or at least much less than us, as our husbands always pay what they can to our families. That's why I don't believe, as you do, in all that the *Rumi* say to flaunt their superiority over us. If you are happy, your sister Nigma is happy, and I am happy with her. But believe me, it's not because of the foreigner that you thrive, but because your good fortune is written in your Destiny, while almost every other woman has it so rough.[18]

***

Things gradually get worse for Gamra, as she falls pregnant and Henry forces her into an abortion, after which he leaves her prostrated on the threshold of their hut to go fight in WWI. Jeanne later finds out that he made it off of the battlefield alive and married a French woman (presumably rich), yet she decides to keep this information to herself, as Gamra's heart is already broken. At the book's end, Gamra finds a little orphan covered in flies and decides to adopt him, and she and Jeanne live together as sisters, raising the happy little boy, who they decided to name Henry.

Leda wrote *The Oasis* in her late forties, and the maturity of her literary style and character development is evident. Unfortunately, it was to be her last published novel, as hard times were on the horizon. Monanni struck up a romance with a woman named Albina Zanini, who had worked on a few projects for the Casa Editrice Monanni, and whom he married in secret, despite his long-standing aversion for civil law and rites. They had a child named Nunzia in 1934, right when Leda's son Aini had his first daughter, Vega. After finding out about Monanni's new marriage and new daughter indirectly, Leda moved out to another apartment on Via Colonna, thus effectively putting an end to her relationship with Monanni and their shared publishing venture. Given the now-tightened fascist control over the press, she focused her literary activity throughout the next decade on writing children's stories for publications that paid contributors, gradually withdrawing from public life entirely.

Italy declared war on Ethiopia yet again in 1935, and the Ministry of Press and Propaganda worked to make sure citizens believed they

---

18   Leda Rafanelli (Etienne Gamalier), *L'Oasi*, 150–152.

"wanted" this war, censoring all air post sent by soldiers in North Africa and working to block the circulation of all propaganda promoting other points of view, even materials printed in English and French.[19] What was left of the opposition had to choose between the revolutionary struggle and the antifascist struggle. The story of the clandestine press in Italy up to and during WWII is largely lost to history, given the extreme secrecy under which operations were conducted. Previous members of the socialist and anarchist fold did join the Italian partisan resistance movement, engaging in direct combat with national armies, as well as infighting amongst themselves. Many others chose to escape from the peninsula entirely.

***

A cool evening descended, after a hot day of sirocco winds. The night would be cold. Henry Nattier sat outside his hut, speaking with somebody in a low voice. He was wrapped in a large, dark colored woolen *bernùs* with a heavy blanket around his shoulders. A white shape, the size of a large dog and halfway hidden under a fold of the thick cloth, crouched at his feet.

The conversation had grown stale. Henry smoked one pungent cigarette after another, throwing the butts into a *gulla* near the stone staircase where he sat. The surrounding grass was burnt by the sun, so dry and arid that a single spark would have easily started a fire.

"No," continued Henry, after a long silence. "I can't remember. I've been in Tunisia since we met in Constantine, and that was only three years ago. I find the natives to be faithfully submissive. They are cheerful and proud to be guided, commanded, and protected by us."

As he spoke, he slowly and tenderly stroked the white shape that rested, without moving and almost without breathing, at his feet.

A sweet, deep voice responded to his claim from beneath the folds of a *bernùs*:

"Not cheerful, nor proud, nor loyal: resigned."

---

19   Maurizio Cesari, *La Censura nel periodo fascista*.

It was a woman's voice.

"If you say so, my friend, I should believe you. You know the natives much better than I do. You speak their language perfectly, and I know you have patiently studied them. You seem to be able to practically intuit their thoughts, as I have seen you do with Gamra. You understand her better than I do. You have penetrated the mysterious soul of these creatures that I find to be sometimes too aloof, other times too loquacious. You do have your ways..."

"I love them, quite simply, and an Arab never betrays love. Which is why everyone calls you an *infidel* and quite rightly so. They know you place no faith in love. You and all of your people only have faith in your ambitions and desires."

The man lit another cigarette. After a long silence, he smiled, observing:

"You speak of us...infidels...as if you were not one of our kind."

"As a matter of fact, after spending thirty years of my life amongst people different from my own kind, without ever being upset by a single quarrel or experiencing the slightest misunderstanding, I have taken on the privilege of citizenship."

"Thirty years! You've been living in Tunisia for thirty years?"

"Thirty years, more or less. I haven't only been in Tunisia, though. I spent time in Algeria, a few years in Egypt, actually, a long time ago. But I've spent most of these thirty years here in Tunisia, between Tabarka, Bone, and the oases. Consequently, I'd say that I understand both the Arab and the East quite well."

"Thirty years!" Henry repeated, nearly incredulous. "Please, Jeanne, forgive me for my indiscrete curiosity..."[20]

---

20   Leda Rafanelli (Etienne Gamalier), *L'Oasi*, 9–11.

CHAPTER VIII
Obscurity

OUR POET (PIETRO GORI)

A Poet doesn't just line words up into verses with rhythmic assonance, or dish out *hermetic* prose devoid of the light of thought. A Poet is an instinctive singer of Life, of Beauty, of Nature, and if the power of a higher Ideal also vibrates within his verses, if his words are illuminated with glints of love and hope for Freedom, then the Poet is worthy of being understood and followed. A Poet is *true* and instinctive when he speaks simply, when he expresses his thoughts, when he exalts human solidarity, when he scorns and condemns the cowardice of those that command and oppress. These free poets create *social* poetry: poetry that does not carve forced words into tempting, tinkling verses, but poetry that makes you think, sending waves of new thoughts through whomever reads or listens to it, rebellious suggestions, an aversion to everything that forms the basis of the social structure, the State, the Church, the Wealth stolen from labor and the sacrifice of the people.

We Anarchists are instinctively Poets, without literary strategies, without academic criticism, we feel the true, free poetry of words expressed with the sincerity of inner thoughts, with an unconscious *purpose* to kindle ideas against the Laws, against the evil that oppresses, against the servile submission of herds of humans, who suffer and endure this oppression.[1]

---

1   Leda Rafanelli, "Il nostro poeta" from *Compagni*, unpublished manuscript, date unknown. Fondo "LR-MM-MLF" conserved at the ABC.

***

Leda moved to Genoa in 1944 in order to be closer to her son and his family; yet Aini suddenly died that same year from peritonitis at the age of 33, leaving behind a widow and three children. Leda spent the next twenty-six years with them in Genoa, seldom leaving her home.

Twenty years of fascism had made it difficult to maintain friendships and business relations with her compagni, and now after the devastating death toll of civilians and soldiers alike, not to mention the absences attributed to those who left the country, few of her friends were still around. Laden with nostalgia, she turned her creative and intellectual focus inwards.

Leda's major late-life project, which she still appeared to be preparing upon her death, was a semi-autobiographical reconstruction of the history of the anarchist movement in early twentieth-century Italy, focusing on her own story and that of her compagni. "If the anarchists don't take care of it, their history will be written by their enemies," as Gaetano Salvemini once said.[2] Indeed, many established institutions would have little interest in preserving the memory of those who fought for a world free from traditional institutions. Pages of drafts show she was in various stages of creating portraits depicting ten of her compagni: Pietro Gori would be introduced with the spotlight on his poetic talents, Giuseppe Monanni, Luigi Molinari, Luisa Minguzzi, Giuseppe Scarlatti, Ezio Bartalini, Ugo Fedeli, Carlo Molaschi, and Luigi Polli would all be included. Weaving biography, history, memoir, and autobiography, she would also describe her own existence in relation to those ideologically and personally close to her.

Excerpts from some of these profiles were printed during the 1960s in *New Humanity* (*Umanità Nova*), a weekly anarchist newspaper founded in 1920 that remains in circulation today. Leda continued making contributions to other newspapers, including *Counter Current* (*Contro Corrente*) and *The Libertarian* (*Il Libertario*), with articles that reflected her continued social engagement, such as *Amusing observations; Today's youth are different; New humanity; Anarchist songs*. Incomplete or unpublished drafts show her developing criticism of the war in Vietnam, the atomic bomb, and the distractive power of television. Others reflect a deeper interest in spirituality and universal harmony.

---

2   Cited in *A-Rivista Anarchica*, year 5 number 42, October 1975. Available at: http://www.arivista.org/?nr=042&pag=42_06.htm.

As mentioned earlier, Monanni, who had been hired as an editorial director at Rizzoli immediately after the war, saw to it that Leda's letters with Mussolini were published in 1946 through the book *A Woman and Mussolini*. This would be the last, full-length book for adult audiences Leda published under her own name during her lifetime, though she dutifully continued with her biography project as well as scores of other manuscripts, many undated and unfinished, written in a wide scrawl that's often hard to decipher.

Despite her withdrawal from public life, Leda began a new career while living in Genoa, developing a word-of-mouth reputation as an excellent palm and card reader. She received her customers in her home, decorated with tapestries and artifacts from North African and Asian cultures. An autobiographical account of her professional experiences and clients was published posthumously in a book titled *Memoirs of a Fortuneteller (Memorie d'una chiromante)*.[3] Aside from the anonymous gossip concerning a few particularly interesting cases, *Memoirs of a Fortuneteller* provides a window into Leda's technique, based on a finely-developed sense of intuition and fully non-nonjudgmental acceptance of the humans who came seeking her help.

In her later years, Leda's personal library had grown to include titles on theosophy, Buddhism, the Baha'i faith, yoga, and vegetarianism. Her continued adherence to the Muslim faith was by no means limiting: rather, it gave her a platform from which she could expand her understanding and her inquiry, into the more mystical aspects of existence.

***

> Every creature is a world in itself. The handprint of every living being is "unique," different from every other, just like every face, body, voice, personality, intellect, and, consequently, Destiny.
>
> [...] All of this evident and proven diversity, among all things and all creatures, creates the great, perfect Harmony, because everything is driven by the same Force, everything evolves and moves, grows and transforms under the same Power. The catalyst, the vital principle is the same for all beings and every thing, from a man to a stone, and is formed from the same substance, obeys the same Laws.

---

3   Leda Rafanelli, *Memorie d'una chiromante* (Cuneo: Nerosubianco, 2010).

Occult, secret laws that are unfathomable to our imperfect minds, to our thick senses, but that govern, guide, and create our Karma, our Destiny.

It's not enough to have goodwill, or tenacity, or even extraordinary intelligence in order to read that Book. One needs to be "adapted to that purpose," to have powers that are not necessarily superior, but are different from those held by people who can not practice this apostolate.

Not everyone, even if they slowly walk across the ground holding a willow branch in their hand, will become a water diviner.

Not everyone, even if they want to enter into spiritual communication with deceased entities, is a medium.

And even when it comes to the more common things in life, if someone doesn't have the aptitude to perform them, they will not reach their goal.

A person with exceptional intuitive abilities, who feels, when near other beings, the irradiation of their individual fluid, is apt to the purpose of probing the future, of advising, of helping someone stay on the path that leads straight to their objective, and not turn around or succumb to wicked passions, and not listen to flattery, but to understand, first and foremost, their full self, their powers, their strengths, their desires; to not falter in their first steps, to not stop when life offers rewards, to never give up hope.

When do you need the advice of a "sheik," or simply an Advisor?

Life is a test, a very easy one for those who, in a karmic sense, have reached an intimate, superior concept of existence—a very difficult one for those who still need to be put to the test, and to whom Fate offers great possibilities to emerge, to thrive, to be in charge of other people.

The sage must never abuse her powers, and even if she feels intellectually superior, must be indulgent and merciful towards the "late-bloomers," just as the strong must be generous and magnanimous with the weak.

The life of humans must unfold based on this intelligent love.

But beyond the great cornerstones of Morality, which all Religions claim to teach and make their followers observe, life arranges, every day, every minute, for every reason, difficult, distressing, impossible, unexpected situations. All living beings, poor or rich, healthy or sick, beautiful or ugly, go through, one after the other, the most mysterious situations, suffer, enjoy, dream, each in their own way, but without understanding the reasons behind what Destiny has assigned to them. When we bend under atrocious pain, when a love that is too violent disorients us, when jealousy tears us apart, when hatred tortures us, when after an offense is inflicted we impulsively and ferociously feel the desire for revenge, then it is wise to seek advice and help from someone who knows more than others.

And also when luck smiles upon us, when fate dispenses its graces, when love makes us happy; even then, the enlightened advice of someone who understands the true and secret meaning of Life must be sought out. Because then it is easier, in the midst of joy and pleasure, to neglect and ignore the soul, as happiness makes us selfish and deaf to the grief of others, and it is truly then that we need not deviate from the way indicated to us, so that we don't lose the good that is not entirely earned.

Our entire Destiny is written in the Great Book of Life and Death: but as very few know how to read it, it is necessary to seek out, in a moment of need, a reliable, trustworthy interpreter.[4]

***

Her granddaughter Marina Monanni says that Leda predicted her own death two nights before she passed away on September 13, 1971, at the age of 91. She had left specific instructions for Marina to dress her in her yellow djellaba, play a recording of Gori's *Farewell Lugano*, and, most importantly, send out a stack of goodbye letters she had written in advance to her friends and the editors of a few magazines she still read or wrote for.

---

4   Leda Rafanelli, *Il nostro destino* (chapbook, date unknown). Conserved in a private collection owned and kindly made available by Fiamma Chessa.

All Marina would have to do was fill in the date and add a thousand lire, Leda's last contribution to the work her compagni carried on.

As she wrote herself in the margins of a manuscript: "Leda isn't the type to ask for directions. She creates her own path herself, and although it twists and turns, it can only be her path."[5] Although there is a romantic aspect to trailblazing, it is by no means easy work. Living faithfully in accordance with one's own, highest principles of freedom, solidarity, and love is no small task, yet it was a feat accomplished with aplomb by Leda.

The majority of Leda's work remains to be discovered, and current plans to publish collections of her writing in Italian provide a promising indication that she will once again be accessible to the general public. Nearly a hundred years after the Italian imperialistic campaigns Leda witnessed as a young woman, the colonial narrative of savage, bloodthirsty peoples living in squalid societies is still used today to justify military inventions in other lands. Oppression of the working class, corruption of religious leaders, marriages for economic security, are all still prevalent: the themes Leda wrote upon in her day can easily be detected in modern society.

On a more theoretical level, her conception of an alternative form of female liberation beyond the paradigm of equality could be expanded in light of recent advances and growing acceptance of an individual's right to define their intimate self, their sexuality, according to rules other than those provided by anatomy, society, or prevalent intellectual trends. And although Leda seemed to have no qualms reconciling anarchism with religion, the question of separating spiritual practice from institutional patronage is still ripe for debate.

Leda Rafanelli specialized in being herself, living authentically, seeking to understand the dynamics of human existence in its freest, most personal expression. The only acceptance she sought was her own, and, accordingly, she was able to draw upon a power and insight that would guide her through a life of challenge, freedom, struggle, and love.

***

I gave myself this name, in addition to the good name I bear, since Djali means: belonging to myself,

---

5   Monnani Marina, *Leda Rafanelli—Carlo Carrà, Un Romanzo: Arte e Politica in un Incontro Ormai Celebre*, edt. Alberto Ciampi, 25.

and I have always belonged only to myself.
Aside from my Mother, nobody in this world has loved me
    as I love me,
since I know all of me, body and soul, heart and mind,
and I understand my every strength and weakness,
as I value myself only for what I'm truly worth:
a lot, in certain situations, not much in others…
But I don't ask myself for anything other than what I can
    give.
I'm not saying I'm magnificent, no; rather, in my case, I've
    always thought
that Destiny, instead of giving me a pretty mask,
wanted to test my intelligence and my strength;
wanted to challenge me with difficult trials in life,
making me fight against the natural
    enemy—Man—disarmed.

It's easy for you pretty, pleasant, attractive women,
with beautiful masks and graceful figures, to submit and
    fall in love, take and keep
the eyes, the heart, the senses of a male…
But I had nothing to my advantage,
nothing that attracts the eye,
neither a beautiful face nor fullness of figure,
no colors, no lights.
And I had to compensate for everything with my ardent
female nature,
with the wisdom to understand and create the great virtues
    of Illusion.

In life I was like a juggler in the piazza,
who makes you think black is white,
who switches the cards with a slight of hand,
who diverts the eyes of others when she doesn't want them
    to see,
who can draw their attention in to a single point,
to produce the desired effect and elicit applause.
I've had nothing, and at times in life I've had everything.

Me, poor, with exotic jewels, precious and rare fabrics,
    mysterious perfumes of the Orient...
Me, ugly, with the most handsome men;
Me, no longer young, with younger males,
—and I kept them around as long as I wanted!—

I've minted false coins and I've bought real gems,
I've thrown Māyā's veil over all the eyes I've loved,
over the eyes I wanted to see me how I wanted to be seen...
And when the enchantment wore off, I knew how to
    disappear...
—But instead of burying myself, I would rise again
since I am Djali, "belonging to myself"—
Every time I loved a man, I only loved the joy he could
    give me,
and He was just a means...just like an object,
since, of men, Allah has created many.

I've loved everything about me, even if Nature didn't give
    me much of a beautiful appearance...
I was able to find things in me that can't be seen...
My hands were able to give much and take much...
My eyes were able to see what others don't see.
In the already gone Past and even beyond the Present, in
    the unknown Future.
I even valued these few centimeters of muscles, bones and
    cartilage,
that we call feet,
that have walked for so long through the streets of the world,
and that—if men would only lift their stupid barriers—
would have taken me, step by step, to Mecca!

I valued the powerful secret behind the virtue of a woman,
who can give and enjoy pleasure in her most intimate fibers,
and loses nothing, but creates
and from a loving kiss gives birth to another living Being,
another human Being,
another Eternal World.

I even loved my own cruel Destiny,
that has taken away everything I ever thought I had,
that has deprived me of all it once gave me,
breaking my heart, only because I loved so much.
But it's my Destiny, and everything that it was
is mine, I love it,
and I wouldn't trade it for another Destiny,
even if it was a happy triumphant Destiny;
just as I wouldn't change my worn and faded, ugly face
for the more beautiful mask of a young woman.

And this is because I know we need to love what is ours,
    only ours;
our skeleton, our soul,
our eyes and our words,
the love inside of us is bigger than all that will be offered
    to us,
our Joy and our Pain.

Now I know that we even need to love our Pain,
—true, agonizing pain—
the most deep, sincere pain—
because our redemption is in Pain,
and Pain releases all guilt...
And at the end of Life, where I've already come,
we'll understand—thinking of our most devastating
    Pain—
how and how much we were able to love.

Leda Djali[6]

---

6   Leda Rafanelli, (Unpublished manuscript, 1 May 1948). Fondo "LR-M" conserved at the ABC.

Sources

The majority of Leda Rafanell's published work and unpublished manuscripts are conserved in two funds: the "Leda Rafanelli—Monanni" ["LR-M"] fund and the "Leda Rafanelli—Marina Monanni—Maria Laura Filardi" ["LR-MM-MLF"] fund, both housed at the Archivio Famiglia Berneri-Aurelio Chessa (Berineri Family/Aurelio Chessa Archives) in Reggio Emilia, Italy. The ABC holds one of the world's largest collections of materials related to the Italian anarchist movement as well as other leftist movements and individuals in Italy and around the world. Its ever-growing collection currently includes over 10,000 monographs and 2,000 periodicals. In addition to organizing events on anarchist history and conservation efforts, it serves as a valuable resource of primary materials for researchers and scholars around the world.

www.archivioberneri.it

Via Tavolata, 6 42121 Reggio nell'Emilia RE Italy

Selected Bibliography

Abou El Fadl, Khaled. *The Great Theft: Wrestling Islam from the Extremists*. New York: HarperCollins, 2007.

Ansaldo, Giovanni. *Gli anarchici della Belle Epoque*. Florence: Le Lettere, 2010.

Antonioli, M; Berti, G; Fedele, S; Iuso, P (directors). *Dizionario Biografico degli Anarchici Italiani*. Volume 1. Pisa: BFS Edizioni, 2003.

———. *Dizionario Biografico degli Anarchici Italiani*. Volume 2. Pisa: BFS Edizioni, 2004.

Aruffo, Alessandro. *Gli Anarchici Italiani, 1870-1970*. Rome: Datanews, 2010.

———. *Donne e Islam*. Rome: Datanews, 2000.

Bettini, Leonardo. *Bibliografia dell'anarchismo*. Volume I, tomes 1 & 2. Florence: CP editrice, 1972.

Bernays, Edward (introduction by Mark Crispin Miller). Propaganda. Brooklyn: Ig publishing, 2005.

Borghi, Armando and Salvemini, Gaetano. *Mezzo Secolo di Anarchia (1898–1945)*. Naples: Edizioni scientifiche italiane, 1954.

Campolonghi, Ernesta. *Femminismo e Socialismo*. Savona: Tipografia Ligura, 1901.

Cerrito, Gino. *Dall'insurrezionalismo alla settimana rossa: per una storia dell'anarchismo in Italia 1881–1914*. Florence: CP, 1977.

Cerrito, Gino (editor). *Malatesta: Rivoluzione e Lotta Quotidiana: scritti scelti del piu famoso anarchico italiano*. Venice: Edizioni Antistato, 1982.

Cesari, Maurizio. *La Censura nel periodo fascista*. Naples: Liguori Editore, 1978.

Chessa, Fiamma (editor). *Leda Rafanelli. Tra letteratura e anarchia. Atti del convegno*. Reggio Emilia: Biblioteca Panizzi, 2008.

Ciampi, Alberto (editor). *Leda Rafanelli—Carlo Carrà, Un Romanzo: Arte e Politica in un Incontro Ormai Celebre*. Venice: Centro Internazionale della Grafica, 2005.

Galleani, Luigi (translated by Sartin and D'Attilo). *The End of Anarchism?* Orkney: Cienfuegos Press, 1982.

Gamalier, Etienne (Leda Rafanelli). *L'Oasi.* Milan: Casa Editrice Monanni, 1929.

Godoli, Ezio (editor). *Il dizionario del futurismo.* Trento: Vallecchi, 2001.

Guidoni, Christiane. "Leda Rafanelli: 'Donna e Femmina.'" In *Chroniques italiennes,* n° 39–40, 1994.

Granata, M. *Lettere d'amore e d'amicizia. La corrispondenza di Leda Rafanelli, Carlo Molaschi e Maria Rossi (1913–1919).* Pisa: BFS, 2002.

Iotti, Laura. *Futuristi e anarchici: Dalla fondazione del futurismo all'ingresso italiano nella prima guerra mondiale (1909–1915)* Carte Italiane, 2(6), 2010.

Lussu, Joyce. *Padre, Padrone, Padreterno: Brevestoria di schiave e matrone, villane e castellane, streghe e mercantesse, proletarie e padrone.* Milan: Gabriele Mazzotta Editore, 1976.

Malagreca, Miguel. "Lottiamo Ancora: Reviewing One Hundred and Fifty Years of Italian Feminism." *Journal of International Women's Studies* Vol. 7 #4 May 2006, pages 69–89.

Malatesta, Errico. *Rivoluzione e lotta quotidiana.* Venice: Edizioni Antistato, *1982.*

———. *Scritti: Volume III.* Geneva: Edizione del "Risveglio," 1936.

Masini, Pier Carlo. *Storia degli anarchici italiani da Bakunin a Malatesta (1862–1892).* Milan: Rizzoli, 1969.

Marshall, Peter. *Demanding the Impossible: A History of Anarchism.* Oakland: PM Press, 2010.

Murtada Mutahhari, Shahid Ayatu 'Llàh (translated by Abdu 'I-Hadi Palazzi). *I diritti della donna nell'Islam.* Rome: Centro culturale islamico europeo, 1988.

Nitti, Francesco. "Italian Anarchists." *The North American Review,* Vol. 167, No. 504 (Nov. 1898), pp. 598–608.

Nurbakhsh, Javad. *Donne Sufi: Storie de donne mussulmane.* Milan: Edizioni Nur, 1993.

Pepicelli, Renata. *Femminismo Islamico: Corano, diritti, riforme.* Rome: Carocci Editore, 2010.

Petricioli, Marta. *Oltre il Mito: L'Egitto degli italiani (1917–1947).* Milan: Bruno Mondadori, 2007.

Rafanelli, Leda. Preface to Albert, Charles. *L'amore libero.* Milan: Casa Editrice Sociale, 1921.

———. *Bozzetti Sociali* (second edition). Milan: Casa Editrice Sociale, 1921.

———. *Una Donna e Mussolini,* second edition. Milan: Rizzoli, 1975.

———. *Donne e Femmine.* Milan: Casa Editrice Sociale, 1922.

———. *L'Eroe della Folla.* Milan: Casa Editrice Sociale, 1920.

———. *Memorie d'una chiromante.* Cuneo: Nerosubianco, 2010.

———. *Per l'idea nostra: Raccolta di articoli e bozzetti di propaganda.* Florence:

Libreria Rafanelli-Polli E C., 1905.

———. *Seme Nuovo*. Milan: Società Editoriale Milanese, 1922.

———. *Vedere il mondo*. Milan: A. Vallardi, 1951.

Sacchetti, Giorgio. "Comunisti contro individualisti, il dibattito sull'organizzazione del 1907." *Bollettino del Museo del Risorgimento*, anno XXXV. Bologna: 1990.

Sarogni, Emilia. *La donna Italiana. Il lungo cammino verso I diritti 1861–1994*. Parma: Pratiche Editrice, 1995.

Scaraffia, Lucetta and Isastia, Anna Maria. *Donne ottimiste: femminismo e associazioni borghesi nell'Otto e Novecento*. Bologna: Il Mulino, 2002.

Stampacchia, Mauro. "L'anarchismo umanista e mondialista di Pietro Gori." Lecture given at the Palazzo Granducale, Livorno, Italy, 2008.

Stirner, Max (translated by Steven Byington). *The Ego and His Own*, 1907. Available online at: http://theanarchistlibrary.org/library/max-stirner -the-ego-and-his-own#toc14.

Tancredi, Libero. *L'anarchismo contro l'anarchia*. Pistoia: Casa Editrice "Rinascimento," 1914.

Wilson, Perry (translated by Paola Marangon). *Italiane: Biografia del Novecento*. Rome-Bari: Edizioni Laterza, 2011.

A few notes on the translations

The excerpts chosen for translation represent but a small fraction of the tens of thousands of pages of work Leda produced during her life, whether published or kept exclusively in the archives in Reggio Emilia. I chose these selections with an eye to presenting topical as well as stylistic variety: this book, however, is not in any way intended to serve as a comprehensive anthology of Leda's work. It merely strives to provide an overview of her work, biography, and historical context.

Translations of Leda's work as well as the Italian citations were performed by the editor. Minor stylistic updates were made, primarily as regards dialogue markings and ellipses, which follow different conventions in written Italian than they do in English. Her capitalizations and italicizations are reproduced faithfully, in order to retain the original emphasis, therefore words such as "Ideas" and "Anarchist" and "State" are intentionally capitalized and not indicative of typographical errors. Leda's use of punctuation and stylistic conventions grew increasingly more creative through the years, as they are much more noticeable and frequently employed from the 1930s onwards (particularly in retrospective pieces or memoirs, such as the manuscript published in *Leda Rafanelli—Carlo Carrà, Un Romanzo: Arte e Politica in un Incontro Ormai Celebre*) than they are in earlier works. An entire study in itself could be performed on the symbolism and significance behind Leda's use of stylistic markers.

Aside from the excerpted sections of *The Hero of the Masses*, which perhaps was produced swiftly or edited in a different manner or not at all, the work chosen for translation tended to be written in clear, easy-to-follow sentence structures and logical arguments. When content is omitted, represented by a [...] before the next section, it is either due to the fact that parts of the original manuscript were missing or illegible, or that such omitted content was specifically related to an argument presented earlier or later in the text that would not be included in the translation, therefore irrelevant to the excerpt and potentially confusing to readers not provided with the additional context.

From a more ideological point of view, Leda's work presents a challenge to the translator as regards words and terms such as *fratelli* (which could be translated as brothers, or brothers and sisters, or siblings), *uomini* (men, or men and women, or human beings). In the case of collective nouns, I wondered whether to reflect the gender bias by including only the male inclusive term, which might be justified by Leda's perspective on gender divisions, or follow a more modern approach and expand the term for a more universal application. I opted for the latter in most cases, given the fact that these terms are often used in works addressed to a general public, and only used a gendered translation when collective nouns for groups of women, sisters, etc. were presented in the same text. The reader should note that this does, however, somewhat compromise the gender bias found in Leda's writing, though it is impossible to tell how much of the bias is due to the constructs of the Italian language and how much is of her own volition.

Index